HISTORY'S BLOODIEST REVOLUTIONS

JOHNATHAN KINGSBURY

RodgerLaz Publishing S.E.N.C.
www.Rodgerlaz.com

Ordering Information:
Quantity sales. Special discounts are available on quantity purchases by corporations, associations, and others. For details, contact the publisher at the address above.
Orders by U.S. trade bookstores and wholesalers. Please contact the publisher at the address above or by email: slazaroff@rodgerlaz.com

Printed in Canada

Publisher's Cataloging-in-Publication data
Johnathan Kingsbury.
History's bloodiest revolutions / Johnathan Kingsbury.
p. cm.
ISBN 978-1-7752921-1-1
1. The main category of the book —History —Other category. 2. Revolutions.

First Edition

14 13 12 11 10 / 10 9 8 7 6 5 4 3 2 1

DEDICATION

Dedicated to my faithful companion, a beautiful black lab named Scipio.

CONTENTS

Acknowledgments   i

Introduction   1

1   Are Revolutions a benefit to society?   13

2   The French Revolution   27

3   The American Revolution   51

4   The Glorious Revolution   75

5   The Russian Revolution   97 71

6   The Iranian Revolution   119

7   The Haitian Revolution   143

8   The Cuban Revolution   167

9   The Taiping Revolution   191

10   The Chinese Revolutions   213

11   The Spanish Civil War   237

12   The Young Turks   261

13   Summary   285

ACKNOWLEDGMENTS

To Kevin, Thank you for all your dedication and help. It was truly a pleasure working with you.

"You say you want a revolution?

Well, you know...

We all want to change the world."

John Lennon / Paul McCartney

INTRODUCTION

The purpose of this book is to examine eleven instances throughout history of 'revolution'. To provide an understanding of the background of these events, the causes and the consequences. But first, let's define what we mean by a revolution.

Meaning of 'revolution'

The etymological origin of the term 'revolution' is from the Latin revolutionem (a revolving) and revolvere (turn or rollback). The word has come to relate specifically to a fundamental change to the status quo and can be applied to all aspects of life. The advent of the microchip brought about a revolution in computer science and subsequently transformed almost every aspect of society through the mass availability of computers. The development of steam locomotion resulted in a revolution of industry and transportation.

This book though is concerned with revolution as a political movement when a population rises up against the current authorities to bring about change to the way they are governed, or in fact to take up the reins of power themselves.

Political revolution

Aristotle defines two types of political revolution;

A complete change from one constitution to another

A modification of an existing constitution

An example of the first kind is the French Revolution whereby the Third Estate (the common people) declared that they and not the nobility or clergy of France were the true leaders of the French state. In a series of violent uprisings, the French working classes overthrew both their rulers and the entire architecture of the French monarchy and aristocracy. France emerged from this period as a socialist republic which would have been utterly unrecognisable to contemporary observers from what had gone before.

An example of the second kind is the 'Glorious Revolution' which occurred in England in 1688 when King James II of England abdicated his throne and subsequently allowed the coronation of William of Orange and his wife Mary (James' grand-niece) to be crowned. With their coronation came the 'Declaration of Right' which outlined the rights of the English people and the rules by which an English monarch agreed to be governed by. This formalised several unwritten conventions which successive English monarchs of the Stuart dynasty had trodden on, and which guaranteed the authority of Parliament over the monarch. The system of government in England remained essentially unchanged except for those guaranteed rights. However, it began the shift of power towards the people's elected representatives in Parliament and that power would remain in their hands to this day.

Further characteristics of a revolution

Aristotle's definition is a good one which fits all of the revolutions which we will examine. But more needs to be added to the definition. To be a revolution it must involve a wide-spread mass uprising of the population. This can be a movement of violence, such as the 'October Revolution' when a mass uprising of the proletariat overthrew the absolute monarchy of Tsarist Russia. It can also be peaceful. An example of this is the 'Velvet Revolution' in Czechoslovakia in 1989 which brought about an end to the one-party Communist state.

A revolution can be viewed differently according to which side the observer is taking if any. A revolution can be viewed as a heroic struggle by a repressed populace to overthrow a tyrannical regime. The revolution may cause considerable violence but this is accepted as necessary to destroy the old regime and bring about the birth of a new order. The American Revolution against the British can be viewed through this lens, a struggle for democracy and liberty against an oppressive Imperialist regime. The 'Arab spring' revolution of 2011 is also generally regarded in this light, ending dictatorships in Tunisia and Egypt and opening the door to democracy.

The opposing view is that revolutions produce chaos as a result of the unleashing of mass anger by a population with grievances against the powers that be. The French Revolution undoubtedly began with the most laudable of intentions but before it was finally ended even the revolutionary leaders had fallen victim to the popular bloodlust they themselves had unleashed. In Libya, the effects of a revolution that overthrew dictator Muammar Gaddafi did not produce a democracy and freedom for the population, but a power vacuum which the revolutionaries were not able to fill due to their own infighting. This allowed for radical Islamists to gain a foothold and the descent of the country into what is effectively a civil war.

Revolutions are far rarer than the instances of injustice and tyranny that give rise to them. History is replete with instances of a downtrodden populace rebelling against the authorities only to be brutally crushed. Most dictators ensure that their power base is secure through control of the military and the means of mass communication. As a result, rebels are often left isolated, vulnerable to being picked off piecemeal. A revolution can occur where it is the government itself which is becoming isolated. This could take the form of a dictator who is out of touch with the suffering of their people. Or it could be one who has alienated those social and political elites who put them into their position.

When the authorities appear to be weak this is when a significant number of people can begin to unite, and more importantly to feel united, against the powers of the state. This belief is crucial. If the people believe themselves to be part of a large-scale movement it lends courage in the face of backlash from the authorities. Observe the mass protests across Egypt in 2011 that brought about the downfall of the long-standing Mubarak regime. This consisted of people who knew, through social media, that they were part of a widespread protest movement and were supported by many millions of others.

Some have argued that to be defined as a revolution there must be a suddenness of action. Events must escalate quickly, over a matter of days or weeks. This is suggested by the word, most people assume a revolution to be a sudden and quick shakeup. While this is the case in some revolutions it is not in all cases. In the revolution that saw Communism sweep China, the revolutionary leader Mao Zedong had spent decades fighting before finally gaining enough momentum and support to take the country as a whole.

This brings us to another aspect of revolution, ideology and social justice. For a revolution to be considered so there will be an ideology driving those who are actively participating in the revolution and a desire for social justice. Social justice can be seen as fairer institutions such as the courts and the democratic process. It can also be the redistribution of wealth and property from the few to the many. Both the 'October' revolution in Russia and the Chinese revolution were the result of a desire for social justice by the masses, underpinned by the ideology of Communism. In these instances, the ideology served as a unifying force which welded together the people under one banner. Had this ideology not existed both revolutions may have fared much worse than they did.

The eleven revolutions chosen for this book fit those characteristics outlined above. History is full of examples of popular uprisings against unfairness, social elites or tyrannies. But not every instance of uprising or regime change can be defined as a revolution.

What a revolution isn't

Peasants Revolts and Grain Riots

For example, the uprising of English peasants in 1381 is a famous example of a peasant's revolt but can't be defined as a revolution. The movement was local in nature, arising in a particular region and not replicated across the entire populace as a whole. There was no fundamental ideology at work behind this uprising or desire to change the constitution. In fact, the rebels were rather seeking the aid of the government to redress their grievances. Peasants revolts have been observed, particularly in the middle ages, in agricultural societies.

In urban areas, there have been many uprisings triggered by food scarcity, usually as a result of rising prices. Examples include the Bread Riots in Boston in 1710, Flour Riots in New York City in 1837 as well as examples throughout the twentieth and twenty-first centuries. Again, these examples of civil unrest cannot be defined as a revolution because they were localised and did not have any overarching ideological drivers.

Coups and Civil Wars

The overthrow of a corrupt regime by a small, elite group would also fall outside the definition of revolution. A coup by military generals to overthrow a corrupt dictator might have all the appearances of a revolution. They may have the mass support of the populace behind them and wish to, and usually, do produce a new constitution. However, these coups are rarely driven by a desire for social justice. The military coup in Thailand in 2006 and then again in 2014 is a good example of this. These coups can be defined as a rebellion. But this is distinct from a revolution. All revolutions start with acts of rebellion. To fit the definition of a revolution though, there must be a desire to change the status quo. One dictator overthrowing another would not be defined as a revolution. By this token, the overthrow of Robert Mugabe in a military coup cannot be said to be a revolution, as it remains unclear whether those responsible intend to simply replace one dictator with another.

A civil war can often lead to a revolutionary war but not every civil war fits the definition of a revolution. Many civil wars are effectively power struggles between rival claimants for power. They usually seek to put themselves into power but to use the institutions and structures of government that already exist, rather than create new ones. This may change where a civil war is triggered by a leader who raises an army to fight for revolutionary principles i.e. social justice, and the overthrow of the old regime in favour of a new constitution. The English Civil War of the 1640's became such a revolutionary war. In this conflict, Parliament fought against King Charles I over the issue of how far the King's power should reach. By the end of the war through the Parliamentary goals had shifted, from removal of Charles I to the abolition of the monarchy entirely. The English Civil War was followed by a complete change to the constitution, though only for eleven years.

INTRODUCTION

Eleven bloody revolutions

The eleven revolutions which this book will examine were not all successful in achieving their aims but all share the characteristic of involving widespread, mass violence and bloodshed in the pursuit of an ideology and desire for social justice. Those chosen are;

1.   The French Revolution - beginning as a series of mass protests over food shortages amongst the French proletariat it resulted in the overthrow of the monarchy, aristocracy and church from 1789 onwards.

2.   The American Revolution - the declaration of independence in 1774 by American colonies belonging to Great Britain. A series of rebellious acts culminated in armed resistance to a British army sent to quell the revolt.

3.   The Glorious Revolution - the name commonly used to refer to the overthrow of the Stuart dynasty which had ruled England and Scotland for almost a century, in 1688. Though the handover of power was bloodless it laid the groundwork for a war between Protestant and Catholic in Ireland which continues to be waged.

4.   The Russian Revolution - an uprising by Russian workers in 1917 to seize control of the state from the autocratic Tsars. Mirroring the French Revolution, a bloody uprising was followed by the violent pursuit of any member of the Russian aristocracy or monarchy and the formation of a brutal Communist dictatorship.

5. The Iranian Revolution - the overthrow of the Iranian monarchy in 1978 - 79 and the establishment of an Islamist state governed by the Ayatollah.

6. The Haitian Revolution - a revolt by slaves on the island of Haiti in 1791 against the white authorities there.

7. The Cuban Revolution - the struggle from 1952 - 1959 by Cuban lawyer Fidel Castro to seize control of Cuba from military dictator General Batista.

8. Taiping Revolution - a revolt in 1851 against the Qing Empire in China which resulted in a fifteen-year war. Inspired by a Chinese Christian mystic claiming to be the brother of Jesus Christ.

9. Chinese Communist Revolutions - a series of rebellions and conflicts which occurred across China from 1911 to 1949 and culminated in the elevation of Mao Zedong to the position of supreme power and China's transformation into a single party Communist state.

10. The Spanish Civil War - a conflict between 1936 and 1939 which captured world attention as a fight between those seeking a democratic republic and the fascist forces of General Francisco Franco.

11. Young Turk Revolution - a revolt in 1908 against the Ottoman Sultan Abdul Hamid III which sought to restore Parliament and bring democracy to the Ottoman Empire.

CHAPTER 1

ARE REVOLUTIONS A BENEFIT TO SOCIETY?

As we've already seen, revolutions can be viewed in different ways according to the standpoint of the observer and the prevailing attitude of the day. Writers such as Thomas Paine and Jules Michelet regarded the American and French Revolutions are heroic uprisings by the masses, led by inspirational men who believed in freedom and democracy. In their view, the violence perpetrated in the cause of this uprising was entirely justified to overthrow the instruments of tyranny and those who would support tyranny.

Thus, by this argument, the American colonists were justified in going to war with the British as they were fighting for their freedom against an unjust ruler and an unjust system of government which would keep them voiceless and oppressed. The French revolution which occurred just over a decade later was part of the same movement towards social justice and freedom. It was, in effect, another tyrannical regime toppled. This view was further developed in the twentieth century by Karl Marx and Vladimir Lenin who formed the belief that revolution by the working classes was inevitable.

It is also possible to view the same events as chaos, unleashed by idealists with good intentions but subsequently running amok. Many English writers criticised the French Revolution for its rampant bloodshed. They claimed that the revolutionary zeal practised against oppressors would, once power had been reached, inevitably be turned inward. Thus, revolutions would tear themselves apart with infighting and power struggles resulting in an even worse suffering of the populace that had been in evidence before. This view, which places the emphasis on the human cost, has been espoused by writers such as Thomas Carlyle and Charles Dickens amongst others.

What are the outcomes of a revolution?

To assess whether a revolution is of benefit to society, we need to look at the outcomes of revolutions. But this isn't as straightforward as it may seem at first. Take the 'Glorious Revolution' in England in 1688 for example.

The immediate outcome of the overthrow of King James II was the accession of a Protestant dynasty to the throne of England and the formalising of a 'Declaration of Right' and 'Bill of Rights' which defined the boundaries of the authority of the monarchy and guaranteed the authority of Parliament. Thus, the arising of an absolute monarch could not happen in England, nor could the elected representatives of the people be dismissed whenever they disagreed with the policies of the Crown (as happened frequently during the reign of James' father Charles I and led to his execution). That would appear to be a positive outcome.

But James tried to retake his throne, doing so with a Catholic army raised in Ireland. The defeat of that army at the Battle of the Boyne in 1690 is celebrated by Protestants in Northern Ireland, Western Scotland and Northern England to the present day. These celebrations have often become violent, triumphalist demonstrations by Protestants over Catholics. Sectarian hatred has been and continues to be a major issue in Northern Ireland and mainland UK cities like Glasgow and Liverpool. Was this the outcome of the Glorious Revolution? A drawing up of battle lines between Protestant and Catholic that continues to this day?

The Russian 'October' revolution is even more ambiguous. It is beyond question that the Romanov dynasty lived in luxury while the working class lived in squalor and poverty. The overthrow of the Tsar brought about an end to this grossly unequal system and a rule by the workers, for the workers. On the surface, this would seem of great benefit and a positive outcome. But what of the Stalinist purges of the 1930's when millions were murdered? Are these the outcomes of the 'October' revolution? Or the decades-long Cold War between the Soviet Union and the United States following the Second World War?

Every revolution clearly has many and varied outcomes. But there are some principles which appear constant.

Time

In each case, there is no immediate outcome which can be assessed. In the destruction of the old regime, it takes time for new revolutionary states to be created and achieve stability. On average this kind of process takes approximately a decade to emerge. During that time it may appear that the result of the revolution has been chaos and upheaval but this is merely the transitional period.

Types of revolution

Revolutions can be categorised into different types, each with its own set of characteristic outcomes.

Social revolutions - typically involve the mass redistribution of wealth and property as an existing social-economic society is completely dismantled to be replaced by the revolutionary system. The revolutions of France, Russia and the Communist revolution of China are all examples of this. Because such a radical redesign of society leads to opposition and counter-revolution, these movements result in highly centralized governments and authoritarian regimes. Once the old regime has been destroyed it is necessary to maintain absolute control over the country to ensure the revolutionary vision can be implemented. Often the ordinary people will enjoy unprecedented health and social care programs as part of this. Rapid economic growth is also seen as a result of a strong central government able to exercise total control over all industries.

Anti-Colonial revolution - where a territory or state is controlled by a foreign power and subsequently rebels in order to gain its independence. Examples of this are the American, Haitian and Cuban revolutions. Once independence has been achieved there is nothing to say this will result in the achievement of the, usually libertarian, ideals which the revolutionaries espoused. The American revolution resulted in a republic which became a world superpower and a champion of individual liberty and democracy. Cuba, however, exchanged one dictator for another (Batiste for Castro). It subsequently suffered decades of economic stagnation as a result of its dictator's choices (Communism) and the sanctions imposed on Cuba by the United States as a result.

Democratising revolutions - these conflicts seek to bring down an authoritarian regime and restore/create a democratically elected government. These movements are often drawn from across a broad social spectrum and are not driven by a single revolutionary leader (such as Fidel Castro). As a result, they are often non-violent (such as the 'Orange' revolution in Ukraine which overturned an election result believed to have been rigged in favour of a Russian puppet). They can also lack the strength of will to go far enough to tear down the old order in pursuit of their own goals. As a result, the revolutionary goals become more diffuse over time and in some cases, there is a return to the status quo. An example of this is the 'Young Turk' revolution of the Ottoman Empire which sought to bring democracy and self-determination to all of the provinces of the Ottoman Empire (something which none of the other Imperial world powers was doing at the time). These goals were never quite achieved however and the revolution was lost amid the chaos of the First World War.

Do revolutions produce democracy?

So, we have seen that revolutions can produce democracies, in place of the regime they overthrow but this is not guaranteed. The French, American and the English 'Glorious' revolutions all either produced stable democracies eventually or strengthened an existing democratic state (in the case of the 'Glorious' revolution). Revolutions are most likely to lead to democracy where there is some prior experience of democracy. In the 2011 'Arab spring' revolts that swept Mediterranean Africa and the Middle East, there was a strong movement for democracy to replace long-standing military dictatorships. In the case of Egypt, this has resulted in a military regime.

Are revolutions good for ethnic minorities and women?

It would seem to be common sense that a revolutionary movement which professes to libertarian ideals of equality and freedom would be supported by, and be good for, ethnic minority groups and for gender equality. After all, it would be paradoxical for a revolutionary leader to proclaim that those who follow him are deserving of freedom from oppression and equality before the law and then deny those principles to others. Many revolutions have promised much but delivered very little.

In the American Revolution much was made of the principle that 'all men are created equal'. One of the battle cries of the revolution was 'give me liberty, or give me death' which would suggest a fundamental belief in equality. One of the principal outcomes of the successful American Revolution was the Constitution and Bill of Rights, which codified the unalienable rights of man. But, famously, this didn't appear to extend to blacks, native Americans or women. Many of the revolutionary founding fathers were slave owners. The fact of slave ownership would be an issue in American politics for the next century and one of the principles which resulted in the outbreak of civil war. Women wouldn't receive the right to vote until 1920. Native Americans would not be recognised as citizens of the United States until 1924 and barred from voting in some states until 1957.

So, the American Revolution did little to further the liberty or equality of women or non-white ethnic groups. It did lay down the groundwork for human rights to which, eventually, all would be recognised as being subject. But this would take almost two hundred years to take effect fully. This is not unusual. There are very few, if any, revolutionary movements in history where once their goals have been achieved it is men who have seized the pivotal roles in the new government.

CHAPTER 1 - ARE REVOLUTIONS A BENEFIT TO SOCIETY?

What are revolutions good for?

So, it would seem that revolutions create chaos and bloodshed in their drive to tear down the old regime and institute a new social order. Often, religious or racial minorities can be ignored in the new regime, receiving no more equality or liberty than they had before. At worst these groups can be actively persecuted (Nazi revolution, Khmer revolution, American revolution). Women never seem to benefit from the libertarian ideals espoused by revolutionary leaders and, historically, have been forced to fight their own battles to achieve equality.

So, what, if anything, are revolutions good for?

Citizenship

A concept created in the ancient Greek city-states, this was at the heart of the American and French revolutions and has become a central tenet of all democracies the world over today. It is rooted in the concept that all people (historically this would have been all men of a certain ethnicity as we have discussed) possess certain human rights which no government can take away. All governments are answerable to the citizenry who elected them and exists to serve that citizenry. This may seem obvious to a modern reader. But contrast this to the single-party states like China or North Korea. Or look back to the constitutional monarchies of the eighteenth century.

These regimes do not take it as read that the citizen possesses equal rights under law than those who govern them. Historically speaking this a relatively new phenomenon. Humanity has far more experience of regimes where it is accepted that certain individuals are superior by birth and this born to rule. So, the principles of the citizen made popular by the American and French revolutions cannot be underestimated or taken for granted. They arose because of revolution.

Socialism

Some would argue that the advent of socialism cannot be seen as a positive. In American politics, and for the past twenty years in UK politics, socialism has been the preserve of radicals on the edge of the mainstream. But the emergence from the French Revolution of the concept that the workers, who constituted the mass of the people, should control the state laid the foundation for the advent of trades unions and workers' rights. In Britain, in the early twentieth century, it led to the formation of the Labour party, a political party formed of and for the ordinary working people.

It sparked the Communist revolutions of Russia and China which many would argue caused untold suffering to many millions of people within and without those countries. But the concept of a political system aimed at representing and improving the lives of ordinary people and not just land-owning elites has improved the lives of just as many. Compare the life of a factory worker in eighteenth-century Manchester to the conditions the same person could expect in the twenty-first. Minimum wage levels, health and safety rules enshrined in law, workers' rights regarding dismissal and fair treatment also protected by law and backed up by powerful trades unions. These things arose as a result of the rise of socialism and it was the socialist revolutions that brought the concept to the mainstream of political life.

Self-determination

Many revolutions have been the result of a desire for self-determination, to break away from a larger and more powerful imperialist state. The American revolution is the perfect example. And it established the concept of self-determination which European imperialist powers would eventually come to agree with. This, in turn, led to the independence of former colonies, with or without bloodshed. So the British agreed to the independence of India, Canada, Australia and New Zealand. The French fought to control Algeria and Indo-Chinese possessions but would ultimately be forced to surrender these territories.

The prevailing view of white imperialist states was that the inhabitants of colonial possessions in Africa and Asia were not capable of self-governing. There was a paternalistic sense that these territories required guidance and leadership. This gave way to a recognition of the right to self-determination. This was replicated in Europe itself, as former Soviet states fought for their independence resulting in revolutionary movements such as the Polish Solidarity movement and the Velvet Revolution in Czechoslovakia, both peaceful revolutions.

Revolutions have given the world the principles which today we hold as central to our concept of civilisation. But they have been achieved at a high cost as will be explored later as we go into the detail of some of history's bloodiest revolutions. The French Revolution cost the lives of a million people, one in twenty of the French population at the time. For the Russian and Chinese revolutions, the death toll was more like one in ten. The Russian revolution and its subsequent enshrinement of Communism at the heart of a world superpower had a further detrimental effect beyond the actual loss of life. It led to fifty years of cold war in which the entire world was forced to divide between east and west. An arms race between Russia and America brought the world to the brink of nuclear holocaust.

No revolution is completely clear of subsequent fallout. The 'Glorious' revolution was set in motion because a Catholic monarch had declared that his infant son would be raised as a Catholic. This led a Protestant Parliament who greatly feared Catholicism to offer the English throne to a foreign prince. The subsequent battle fought by James II to recover his throne has been the linchpin of sectarian violence in Ireland and the United Kingdom for the next four hundred years. Even today there are parts of the UK where Protestants and Catholics regard each other with open hatred.

The American Revolution failed to address the issue of slavery or the rights of non-white inhabitants of America. This, in turn, paved the way for a bloody civil war, one of the bloodiest conflicts in which the United States has ever been involved. The issue of race remains polarizing today in America.

So, while it is clear that revolutions can be of great benefit to the societies which have endured them there is also a cost in each case. And that cost continues to be paid for many generations to come.

CHAPTER 2

THE FRENCH REVOLUTION

Introduction

The French Revolution lasted for a decade from 1789 to 1799. It saw the complete overthrow of the French monarchy, aristocracy and the Catholic church in France. In place of these institutions emerged a republic which enshrined the principles of liberty, equality and democracy. The revolutionary chaos was effectively ended in France by the rise to power of general Napoleon Bonaparte and his assumption of supreme power over the newly forged French Empire.

The revolution heralded a seismic shift in European politics, rejecting the concept of privilege due to birth which had been the cornerstone of the feudal system over the last thousand years or more. The authority of the church was also rejected and the liberal philosophies of 'Enlightenment' thinkers such as Voltaire, Rousseau and Paine were embraced. Concepts such as citizenship and the unalienable rights of man replaced ideas such as the divine right of kings and nobility to rule. The French Revolution would serve as an inspiration for other revolutionaries the world over. The motto of the 'Young Turks' who sought to overthrow the absolute rule of the Ottoman Sultans was an echo of the French Revolutionary war cry.

The revolution was an orgy of violence and bloodshed, with royalty and aristocrats publicly executed. Revolutionaries then turned on each other, purging their ranks of supposed traitors to the cause in a series of bloody power struggles. The upheaval of the 1790's was brought to an end with the advent of Bonaparte, who restored order. But what then followed was almost fifteen years of war and conquest as he sought to expand the French Empire across Europe. The revolutionary wars ultimately spread the revolutionary ideals across Europe.

2.1 - The Ancien Regime

To gain an understanding of the French revolution and its causes it is first necessary to examine pre-Revolutionary France. This period is known as the 'ancien regime', quite literally 'the old regime'.

Louis XVI ascended to the French throne on the 10th May 1774. He inherited a country on the verge of bankruptcy. France had fought in the Seven Years War in the late 1750's and had lent its support to the American revolutionaries during the American fight for independence from the British. These two conflicts had cost the French treasury dear and required drastic measures. Louis and his ministers proposed numerous means to achieve this including tax reforms that placed more of the tax burden on rich aristocrats than on the French peasantry, and curtailing of privileges enjoyed by both aristocracy and clergy. The reforms failed in the face of deeply entrenched self-interest on behalf of these two elements of French society.

The ancien regime was a realm in which the peasants carried on their backs the aristocracy, clergy and monarchy. It was the ordinary peasant class who worked to produce but they were also subject to the largest tax burden. One way in which Louis XVI sought to address this was by the abolition of the 'taille' which was a land tax payable only by non-nobility. By contrast, the aristocracy and clergy of France had numerous exemptions to enable them to avoid taxation. To make matters worse, the privileges enjoyed by the French elite were protected by the parlements, a court system whose judges held a vested interest in maintaining those privileges.

Because of the entrenched power of the parlements, Louis was unable to implement any of the reforms which would have made life more tolerable for the French peasantry. He had sought to abolish serfdom (whereby peasants worked land owned by the nobility and for the nobility - effectively making them the property of the landowner) and introduce toleration for non-Catholics. Ironically, the determination of the clergy and the nobility to hold onto the privileges threatened by these reforms would lead to the loss of all privileges when the peasantry finally found their voice and revolted.

2.2 - The Estates-General

Unable to achieve economies or persuade the parlements to agree on tax reform, Louis was forced to call an Estates-General in May 1789. It was the first time since 1614 that the body had been summoned. The Estates General was a body consisting of elected representatives of the Three Estates which French society was comprised of; Clergy, Nobility and the Third Estate, representing the working class who made up ninety-five percent of the French population. Precedent held that each of the Estates would meet separately with the First and Second Estates able to vote down the third.

The representatives of the Third Estate numbered double that of the First and Second but the deputies were informed that all voting within the Estates General would be 'by power' not 'by headcount'. In other words, as precedent dictated, the majority numbers of the Third Estate would be meaningless, their voice would not be heard. This led many of the middle-class Third Estate deputies to meet separately from the rest. The Third Estate deputies were not willing to be silenced. For this meeting of the Estates General they, in particular, were extremely well motivated. The common people of France had been inspired and saw the Estates General as their opportunity to effect change. That inspiration came from a writer.

One of the elected representatives of the Third Estate was Emmanuel-Joseph Sieyes, a former clergyman who became a political writer. His pamphlet, published in January 1789, 'What is the Third Estate?' would become the manifesto for the Revolution with around 30,000 copies printed in the first few months of its publication. In this work, Sieyes asked what the third estate was currently, and provided the answer 'Nothing'. He then asked what the Third Estate wished to be, and provided the answer 'Something'. Sieyes view was that if the First and Second Estates were allowed to continue in their current form the Third Estate was destined to remain as nothing.

On the 17th June, the members of the Third Estate declared their assembly to be the only true voice of the French people and named themselves 'The National Assembly'. They invited the other two estates to sit with them in the Assembly but only as equals. On the 20th June, the members of the new Assembly found that they had been locked out of the building in which the Estates General were meeting. They relocated to a nearby tennis court and there took an oath (known as the 'Tennis Court Oath') that they would not disperse until France had been given a new constitution, from which the nobility and clergy would be expressly excluded.

2.3 - The Revolution begins - The Fall of the Bastille

The emergence of the National Assembly and the swearing of the 'Tennis Court Oath' marked the beginnings of the Revolution. The first act of violence was soon to follow. There was unrest in Paris following food shortages and subsequent riots in 1788. Louis XVI brought in soldiers to maintain order but this was seen by the new National Assembly as a threat. The electors of Paris (those who chose the representatives who would sit in the Estates-General for the Third Estate) raised a militia of 40,000 to protect the Assembly. On the 14th July, in search of gunpowder and cannon, they marched on the Bastille. The Bastille was an arsenal as well as a notorious Paris prison, particularly for political opponents to the monarch. Prisoners of the Bastille had included, amongst others, the liberal writers Voltaire and Diderot, both of whom as members of the Enlightenment movement had been hostile to the ancien regime.

The governor of the Bastille resisted and the fortress was stormed. Both the governor and the chief magistrate for Paris were lynched, their heads placed on pikes. It was to be a grisly presage of the violence to come. It was also an extremely important symbol of the birth of the revolution. Amongst ordinary Parisiens the Bastille was a symbol of the oppressive power of the state. Its fall was heralded as a triumph both by the revolutionary leaders and by liberals around the world. To this day Bastille Day is a day of holiday and celebration in France.

2.4 - The end of the Ancien Regime

The National Assembly now dubbed itself the Constituent Assembly and set to work drafting the first constitution of France. It issued a series of decrees between the 4th and 11th August 1789 that removed the administration of the Ancien Regime. The feudal system was abolished as was the system of privilege. The paying of tithes (Church taxes) was abolished as were all taxes or rents due to be paid by peasants to noble landowners. Seigneurial law courts were abolished (these were courts in which the local landowner acted as a judge) as was all exemption from taxation to which the nobility and clergy had previously been able to claim.

The Constituent Assembly's decrees laid out a new vision of the state founded on the principle of equality. There would be equality before the law, social equality, equal liability to taxation and equality of opportunity (meaning that all offices of state would be open equally to all men regardless of their birth). To this point, the nobility had maintained a monopoly on all high offices of state and had thus been able to guarantee their own rights and privileges. All of this was now swept away.

The only area where equality did not yet reach was gender. The Assembly had no interest in ensuring equality between men and women. The decrees referred to the men of France only. On the 26th August 1789, the founding principles of the revolution were gathered together to produce the 'Declaration of the Rights of Man'. This document consisted of seventeen points which codified the basic, unalienable rights of men. Amongst these rights was freedom from arbitrary arrest and the assertion that the source of sovereignty lies in the nation, not the monarch. Thus the Louis XVI went from being an absolute monarch to one who ruled by the consent of the people, a constitutional monarch.

In pursuit of equality, on the 19th June 1790, all nobility was abolished. By this degree, no longer would any man be entitled to hold any title (such as Prince, Duc, Comte etc.). The decree went on to abolish the livery of aristocracy and require that all men should be known by their family names only. However, this stage of the revolution was moderate compared to what was to come (though revolutionary compared to what had gone before it). The decree of 19th June was careful to ensure that property rights were maintained. No citizen was allowed to seize or destroy property belonging to the former nobility of church under the pretext of equality.

Those who had passed these decrees were educated commoners, aided by some liberal nobles and clergymen. They were moderate in their desire to see France as a constitutional monarchy, with the powers of the King held in check by an elected body that held true power. Their primary concern was the orderly transition to the new regime. But they were increasingly out of step with the millions of ordinary people who, encouraged by the first stirrings of revolution were becoming increasingly impatient for real change and improvements to their lives.

2.5 The radical revolution - Jacobins and Girondins

In Paris, in particular, there was a large scale series of mass protests. Leading these protests were the lower middle class including tradesmen, shopkeepers and artisans who were known as the Sans Culottes because they wore trousers instead of the knee breeches favoured by the nobility. They were the organisers of street violence and demonstrations in Paris and forced the pace of change beyond what the Assembly had envisioned.

There was also a schism opening within the revolution itself. The moderates within the Assembly wanted to go no further than the creation of a constitutional monarchy but this required the cooperation of the King. However, the royal family were implacably opposed to the revolutionary ideals. In particular, the King's younger brothers, the Comte de Provence and Comte de Artois and Queen Marie-Antoinette. Both of the King's brothers fled France and were actively fermenting counter-revolutionary movements outside of France with the view to restoring the ancien regime with foreign military support. Marie-Antoinette, sister of the Hapsburg emperor also believed that force was the only solution.

In June 1791 the Royal family attempted to flee to the French eastern border where they could re-negotiate with the Assembly with foreign military aid. They were intercepted at the town of Varennes and returned to

Paris. The moderates were faced with a king who was publicly hostile to their cause and increasingly vocal radical groups such as the sans-culottes mobilising the people in the streets of Paris. The capture of the French Royal family at Varennes and their effective imprisonment subsequently made the issue of the Revolution an international one.

Following the capture of the Royal family, an open letter was published, from Leopold II, Emperor of Austria to Catherine II of Russia. It deplored the treatment of the French royal family and expressed concern for their safety. Another document made public at this time was the Declaration of Pillnitz by the monarchs of Austria and Prussia, calling for the support of all European monarchs in military intervention against France. In April 1792 France declared war on Austria and invaded the Austrian Netherlands (Belgium) with the avowed aim of liberating their fraternal brothers in that country.

Amongst the members of the Assembly, there would have been an increasing feeling of being under attack from all quarters. The monarchs of Europe were gathering to destroy the revolution, the moderates were attempting to bargain with an untrustworthy king who would see foreign troops enter France to undo the Revolution. Seated on the left of the Assembly was a number of radical deputies known as the Jacobins of which the foremost was Maximilien de Robespierre. In September 1791, the National Assembly dissolved itself in order to make way for a new Legislative Assembly. Robespierre suggested that men who had sat in the National Assembly should be barred from election to the Legislative Assembly. This was agreed and signalled the death knell of the moderates.

Robespierre and his fellow left-wing radicals were supported by Jacobin clubs across the country. Thus when it came to elections for the new Assembly they were able to mobilise effectively. Half of the deputies to the new Legislative Assembly were under 30 and radically-minded. In the streets, the freedom of speech guaranteed in the Declaration of the Rights of Man had led to an outpouring of radical opinion into newspapers which served to fire up the public and in particular the sans-culottes. These papers regularly attacked the symbols of the ancien regime, the priests, nobility and the royal family. But they also targeted what they described as 'active citizens', namely those working in the administration created by the National Assembly.

Within the new Assembly, the Jacobins were growing in voice and strength, supported by another radical group, the Girondins. When the King vetoed a proposed measure for a 20,000 militia levy to protect Paris, it was the Girondins who called for a mass demonstration at the Tuileries (the royal palace in Paris). On the 10th August, an armed mob of sans-culottes broke into the palace and slaughtered the King's guards, who Louis had ordered not to open fire. The royal family were taken the prisoner and held in a fortress in Paris. It was the death knell of the constitutional monarchy.

2.6 - War and the abolition of the monarchy

The Revolution had so far found itself split on the issues of the church, the King and now the war. Between July and September 1792, Prussian troops had advanced onto French soil, capturing the border fortress of Verdun. The moderates wished for a reformed Catholic church and monarchy. The radicals wanted the abolition of both and now they had the upper hand. With the threat of invasion looming, panic reigned in the streets of Paris and the sans-culottes began a persecution of the perceived enemies of the revolution; namely, priests and 'counter-revolutionaries'. In the 'September Massacre,' many were taken from the prisons of Paris and murdered in the streets.

On 20th September 1792, Robespierre and the Jacobins successfully brought about the dissolution of the Legislative Assembly which had brought them to prominence. In its place was created a National

Convention. It was this Convention which on the 22nd September, abolished the monarchy. The Republic of France had been created. In January 1793, accused of crimes against the nation, Louis XVI was found guilty and executed by guillotine. His queen would follow in October.

By 1793 the situation in France looked grim for the survival of the revolution. A coalition of nations (Britain, Prussia, Austria, Holland, Spain and Sardinia) was now actively at war with France and invading from, literally, all directions. As well as this there were counter-revolutionary rebellions springing up all over France though particularly focused on Normandy and Brittany and the Vendee region. The response to this was the levee en masse which the Convention issued in August 1793 and called for 750,000 men to be called up for the army. It also called upon the harnessing of all human and material resources for the revolution and the war. In effect, this was the beginning of 'total war', where a nation devotes every aspect of itself, population and economy, to mobilisation for war. It would be a familiar concept by the twentieth century but it was born in August 1793.

France was at war and also in the grip of a civil war with Bordeaux, Lyons and Marseilles erupting into armed rebellion against the revolution and Toulon defecting to the British. Even the radically domination Convention was not unified. The Girondins were removed from power in May 1793 by the machinations of Robespierre and the Jacobins. They formulated a new constitution, to replace the constitution created in 1791 by the Convention. But the 1793 constitution was immediately suspended while France remained at war. The government fell to the Committee of Public Safety, comprising twelve members of the Convention. The period over which this war government presided came to be known simply as The Terror.

2.7 - Robespierre & The Terror

The chief agents of revolutionary zeal were the sans-culottes and they became the symbol of the true revolutionary. They wore the red cap of liberty, and when they stormed the Tuileries palace in September 1792 forced the king to wear it. The sans-culottes addressed all they encountered as 'citizen' and were likely to report anyone choosing to use any of the traditional forms of address (such as Monsieur). They made up the majority of the watch committees which had been created to ensure that counter-revolutionaries were rooted out of society. It was the mass of the sans-culottes who could be whipped up into a killing frenzy when the Jacobins required it. Eighty thousand armed sans-culottes had helped in the overthrow of the Girondins. It is the image of the sans-culottes which is instantly recognisable in our modern times as a symbol of the revolution.

The period known as the Terror saw the creation of 'revolutionary tribunals' supported by a 'revolutionary committee' or 'watch committee' with the avowed purpose of stamping out counter-revolutionaries. These committees were staffed by Jacobins and sans-culottes. Members of the National Convention travelled the country to reassert the control of the Convention over outlying areas. This was in contrast to the devolution of powers which had been created by the moderate revolution in 1789. This wasn't the only element of the moderate revolution which was undone by the Jacobins. The Declaration of the Rights of Man, a key revolutionary document, was suspended. Meanwhile, any applicant for public office had to possess a certificate verifying their revolutionary character. Possession of this certificate became law with the passing of the Law of Suspects in September 1793 which allowed for indefinite imprisonment. By this law, around 500,000 men and women were arrested and detained.

In a decree passed by Robespierre in June 1794 declared the rights of the tribunal to punish the enemies of the people. Suspects were allowed no legal representation and were not allowed to call witnesses. To be accused was to be assumed guilty and the conviction rates were around seventy-five percent. Amongst those deemed to be enemies of the people were Georges Danton, a Jacobin who had served as Minister of Justice. The Girondins were also targeted as enemies of the people. From September 1793 to July 1794 approximately 17,000 people were sentenced to death by the tribunals, the majority for the crime of being as counter-revolutionary.

An estimated 40,000 people died during the Terror. These included approx. 12,000 summary executions without trial, 12,000 deaths in jail awaiting execution as well as those 17,000 sentenced by the tribunals following trials. Robespierre was the primary motivator for the execution of counter-revolutionaries. Driven by his zeal acts of shocking cruelty were carried out in regions of counter-revolutionary insurrection, with the 'representatives on a mission' carrying the rabid revolutionary zeal to the regions beyond Paris. In Lyon, firing squads were used because the two minutes per person rate of execution via the guillotine was deemed too slow. In the Vendee, mass drowning in the Loire River.

The Terror peaked with the Great Terror which took place over a seven-week period from June to July 1794. In this period alone, 1400 people were guillotined in Paris, which was more than in the previous year.

The Convention, under Robespierre's control, did more than simply enact brutal reprisals against those who opposed it. Their intent, driven by the zealous Jacobins, was to see the ancien regime uprooted in every sense from French society. This went further than the overthrow of a monarch and the implementation of a new system of government. While the tribunals were hunting for counter-revolutionaries, there were other changes to be made to the religion of France and the calendar.

The Catholic church was not compatible with revolutionary ideas and it was a symbol of the ancien regime. Sans-culottes exhumed the bodies of former French kings, to rebury them in a common grave. Churches were vandalized or destroyed and those priests who had already fled the country were persecuted and executed. The sans-culottes ensured that churches were not re-opened. Street and place names were changed to remove any Catholic overtones and first names with biblical origins fell out of favour.

Catholic saints days and religious festivals were replaced with revolutionary public festivals designed to imprint into the public consciousness the names of men who had given their lives to the revolution. They sought to create a new pantheon of revolutionary saints, to be immortalised in place of those who came from the old Church. Two of the great philosophers of the Enlightenment movement which had inspired the revolution (Voltaire and Rousseau) were re-interred amid great veneration as heroes of the people and prophets of the revolution. In November 1793 the great symbol of Catholicism in France, Notre Dame cathedral was re-consecrated at the Temple of Reason.

Finally, in May 1794, the Convention passed a decree instituting a cult of the 'Supreme Being'. Robespierre himself celebrated the first 'Festival of the Supreme Being' held in June 1794. In 1795 a decree formally separated church and state in France.

Another area of change was the calendar. Revolutionaries wanted to discard anything that was a reminder of the ancien regime, including all references to history and myths. They instituted a ten month year and a ten hour day. This included renaming days, months and even the hours of the day, though even the dictatorial Robespierre couldn't force ordinary French people to adhere to this. At best the changes made to the calendar and the decimalisation of time was a paper change to demonstrate to history the ambitions of the revolution to make a complete break with the past.

2.8 - Downfall of the Jacobins and the end of the revolution

In July 1794 there was a coup against Robespierre and the Jacobins. It was perpetrated by deputies in the Convention who had come to believe that the fanatical violence of the Terror had gone too far. Many deputies who did not follow the radicalism of the Jacobins were afraid for their lives, fearful of being branded enemies of the people if they did not support every action taken by the Jacobins. Robespierre was arrested and executed by guillotine along with a hundred others. Those who had overthrown him became known as the 'Thermidorians' as Thermidor was the name of the revolutionary month that had replaced July. The Thermidorians put an end to the trials of the tribunals and the mass executions. Using the army they brutally suppressed the sans-culottes, who since the beginnings of the revolution had been a powerful force for radicalism.

The entire governmental system of the Terror was dismantled. A bicameral legislature was formed consisting a 'Council of 500' and a 'Council of Elders'. The universal male suffrage was rescinded, removing power from the hands of the sans-culottes. Now, only landowners were permitted to vote. This covered educated men who had taken lands seized from the church, and former nobles who had given up their rank and privileges and joined the Third Estate in 1789.

It would appear as though the revolution was over but it had merely changed its form. The revolutionary ideals of equality and democracy were still held dear and present at the heart of the constitution. But they were no longer being spread within France by the masses. The politicized sans-culottes had been put in their place and the 'natural' ruling classes were once more in charge. The revolutionary zeal which under the Jacobins was directed towards rooting out enemies of the people was now turned to spreading the revolutionary message by violence. It had long been the ambition of the revolutionary commanders to expand the French frontier to the 'natural' border of the River Rhine. France had many enemies among the traditional monarchies of the rest of Europe and would continue to fight, to preserve the revolution and spread it.

The wars which raged from 1792 - 1797 became known as the Wars of the First Coalition, referring to the coalition of Britain, Prussia, Austria and Spain which sought to invade France and restore the monarchy. Despite initial successes and making inroads into French territory the Coalition was defeated separately, each making their own treaties with France. From 1797 - 1802 the Wars of the Second Coalition saw another attempt to restore the French monarchy but in contrast to their previous objectives, the Coalition now sought to contain the expansion of the French Republic, rather than simply invade and remove the revolutionary government.

One of the reasons for the change in the nature of the conflict from 1792 to 1797 was the rise to command of Napoleon Bonaparte. Bonaparte had risen to become one of France's most successful generals and was turning the tide of the war which, in 1792 must have seemed impossible. By 1799 a new constitution was drafted which granted supreme power to Bonaparte. The constitution was written by Emmanuel-Joseph Sieyes, the man whose writing had so driven the Third Estate to revolution in 1789. The intention was to bring stability to the country, following the chaos the revolution so far, as well securing France's borders and carrying the message of the revolution abroad. Of the two chambers created in the 1795 Thermidor constitution; the lower house was disbanded in October 1795 for its royalist sympathies. Bonaparte disbanded the upper chamber on the 9th November 1799. On the 15th December 1799, Bonaparte declared that the revolution had now been established on the principles with which it began. 'It is over' he said.

2.9 – Summary

The French Revolution began with a monarch desperate for money and aristocratic and clerical classes refusing to surrender their privileges and happy for almost all of the burden of taxation to fall onto the shoulders of the peasants. When Louis XVI summoned the Estates-General in 1789 he found the Third Estate (the elected representatives of the peasant class) had been politicised and radicalised by the writings of Enlightenment philosophers such as Voltaire and Rousseau, who preached of liberty and equality. The complete intransigence of France's ruling elite to surrender any part of their vested interests led to the Third Estate seizing the reins of power from them.

The decrees of the 1789 National Assembly bound the monarch into a constitutional government and eliminated all discrimination and preference based on birth or rank. To a modern, liberal politician the 1789 constitution probably looked just and proper as the constitution for a liberal democracy. Unfortunately, the revolution did not end there. As dispossessed clergy and nobility tried to undermine the revolution, and the monarch appeared to conspire with foreign powers to restore his place, the mass of the French people became a mob capable of imposing its will. As the violence grew in the streets, radicals within the Assembly engineered the downfall of the moderates from 1789 and the beginning of a purge of anyone deemed to be an enemy of the people.

Under Robespierre and his Jacobin extremists, some 40,000 were executed as enemies of the state. Rule of law was suspended and a reign of terror gripped the country for a year until the Jacobins could be purged from the government. During this time, the extremes of the revolution had so outraged the monarchies of Europe that a coalition of powers was set on invading France and restoring the monarchy. They never succeeded but the war which began in 1792 as an attempt to conquer France waged until 1815, with the final defeat of Napoleon Bonaparte at Waterloo. The wars which

France fought from 1792 to 1815 were the first of what would become a familiar sight to history, the 'total war'. This was a war from which none could hide. Warfare was longer practised between two armies, it involved the total population and economy of a country. To achieve victory over the Coalition France was forced to recruit en masse and turn its entire economy over to the war effort. By the time the Napoleonic Wars were over the estimated combined death toll, for civilians as well as combatants was over 3.5 million.

CHAPTER 3

THE AMERICAN REVOLUTION

Introduction

The American Revolution occurred between 1765 and 1783 and consisted of the struggle by the thirteen British colonies established in North America, to free themselves from rule by the Crown. It began as a desire for governance with equal representation in Parliament as those living on mainland Great Britain enjoyed and became a desire for outright self-determination. The colonies in question had been established along the eastern coast of North America and were;

- Delaware

- Pennsylvania

- New Jersey

- Georgia

- Connecticut

- Massachusetts Bay

- Maryland

- South Carolina

- New Hampshire

- Virginia

- New York

- North Carolina

- Rhode Island & Providence Plantations

The inhabitants of the North American colonists (excepting native Americans) were regarded as British subjects and were subject to taxation by the Crown as such. But they had no voice in the British democratic system and no representation in the House of Commons. From 1765 onwards a series of protests took place against this policy, culminating in British retaliation. This spurred the colonies to reject Crown rule and create their own independent state governments. In April 1775 the revolution exploded into open warfare. The colonists raised militia with which to fight the mighty professional army of the British and until 1778 they struggled alone in this fight. The revolutionary war widened into a world war when France declared war on Britain, in alliance with the Americans. This brought France's allies, Spain and the Netherlands into the conflict and helped turn the tide of the revolutionary war.

The North American colonists were ultimately victorious and the war ended with the Treaty of Paris in 1783. What followed would ultimately transform world politics. The American nation rejected the old European concepts of aristocracy, privilege and social class in favour of a social system which, on the surface at least, was egalitarian. A system of government was devised that would prevent the arising of a dictator as well as the danger of 'mob' rule, with checks and balances to ensure the independence of executive, legislature and judiciary. This was guaranteed by a written constitution created in 1789 which has only been amended twenty-seven times in the last two hundred years.

The first ten of these amendments, made between 1777 and 1778 constitute the Bill of Rights, which guarantees individual civil liberties and certain unalienable rights (freedom of speech, freedom of religion etc.). These two documents were amongst the most revolutionary social and governmental concepts of the era. Their example would inspire the revolutionaries of France and would serve as a beacon of liberalism and democracy. Of course, these rights and freedoms were only deemed to apply to white, European descended men. A significant number of the leaders of the American Revolution were owners of black slaves. No mention of these slaves was made and this issue, unresolved at the time of independence would result in a much bloodier conflict a century later as the fledgeling United States was torn apart by civil war.

To further consider the American Revolution we will begin by looking at the origins of the colonies and the state of affairs leading up to the revolution

3.1 - The Thirteen Colonies

The British colonies in North America were established between 1601 (Virginia) and 1732 (Georgia). They were founded as a combination of mercantile ventures and havens of religious tolerance and freedom. Many of the New England colonies were settled by Puritans seeking either to split from or reform the Church of England and seeing the opportunity of creating a new church for themselves in the New World.

Other colonies, such as the colony of Virginia was founded in order to produce raw materials that could be exported. All of the North American colonies would ultimately become rich sources of trade for the British Empire, which relied for its power and wealth on the trade generated by its huge merchant navy. Britain's economic policy demanded overseas colonies capable of importing manufactured goods from Britain and exporting raw materials such as cotton, tobacco, timber and gold. As such the North American colonies were of great economic value to the British Empire, which by the 1770's was one of the world's foremost imperial powers.

There was competition for the natural wealth of North America from both the Spanish (whose North American empire had been forged from the west coast after conquering Central America and Mexico) and the French (whose territory bordered the British colonies immediately to the west. Life in the North American colonies was difficult. The settlements had to be created out of the wilderness and sometimes against the hostile opposition of natives. Diseases to which Europeans had never been exposed were rife, particularly in the hot and humid climate of the southern colonies such as Georgia and Virginia.

The colonists were a broadly homogenous group of English speaking, British born Protestants. They found themselves fighting to tame a wilderness against difficult odds, opposed by other nations as well as nature. In this environment and given all that they already had in common it is no surprise that they were able to unify so effectively when threatened.

3.2 - The French - Indian War and the Stamp Tax

The war which is known to Americans as the French-Indian War was an extension of what in Europe was known as the Seven Years War. In North America, the conflict pitted British colonists and their Indian allies against the French and their own native allies. The conflict is notable for having been triggered in North America by an attack by British colonists led by a young George Washington against a French patrol in May 1854. The war in North America was principal to gain control of the Ohio Valley.

British troops were sent to support the approximate 1.5 million British colonists who had established settlements from Nova Scotia in the north to Georgia in the south. The conflict raged from 1754 to 1763 when it was brought to an end by the Treaty of Paris. By this time the French had lost Canada and ceded their territories west of the British settlements. The Spanish had also ceded Florida, leaving Britain as the single European power with a significant presence in North America.

But the war had been extremely costly to Great Britain which now sought to reclaim some of its costs. The first measure introduced was the Stamp Tax, in 1765. This consisted of a decree that all printed materials in the colonies should use specially stamped paper imported from Britain, containing a revenue stamp. It was argued that the revenue raised from this measure was needed to maintain garrisons of British troops to protect the colonies. The colonists disagreed with this rationale. They argued that the garrisons were not necessary and furthermore that to tax without consent was against their fundamental rights. It is at this time that the phrase 'No taxation without representation' became a popular rallying cry.

In answer to British attempts to collect taxes from their North American colonists, protest groups sprang up throughout the colonies, calling themselves 'Sons of Liberty'. They attacked British tax collectors, often tarring and feathering them, burning effigies of them and disturbing the act of collecting taxes. Their activities were centred around Boston, which became the hub for protests. In October 1875, a meeting took place that was a first for the colonies. It became known as the Stamp Act Congress and it was an assembly of representatives from all thirteen colonies. The meeting took place in New York City and resulted in a petition being sent to Parliament objecting to the new tax.

The petition and the protests had an impact as did lobbying from British merchants who found American colonists boycotting their goods. Parliament repealed the Stamp Act on March 18th, 1766.

3.3 - The Townshend Acts

Though it had conceded the unpopular Stamp Tax, Parliament did not concede it's right to tax the North American colonists. In 1767 a series of Acts was passed which collectively were known as the Townshend Acts, after the then Chancellor of the Exchequer, Charles Townshend. The first of these was the Revenue Act, an indirect tax on certain British imports that colonists were not allowed to buy from anywhere else (paper, glass, lead, paint and tea). It was followed by the Commissioners of Customs Act and the Vice-Admiralty Courts Act all in 1767. All were deeply unpopular with the colonists. The Commissioners of Customs Act created an independent body answerable to the British Admiralty was responsible for the policing of trade regulations, preventing smuggling and ensuring all duties were paid. These Commissioners became notorious for their corruption. The Vice-Admiralty Courts Act allowed for the better prosecution of smugglers by creating four new Vice Admiralty Courts to service the colonies (previously there had only been one). It was unpopular because the trade restrictions and taxes they enforced were regarded by most Americans as unfair and unjust.

Resentment brewed against the new legislation and Boston was the heart of the growing anger. It prompted the British to station troops in the city to maintain order. On March 5th, 1770 a large mob confronted a group of British sentries resulting in shots being fired into the crowd and five deaths. On the 12th of April 1770, the Townshend Act was repealed, though this was too close to the events of the Boston Massacre for the deaths to be the cause of this u-turn. But one vital taxation was retained from the discarded Acts. A tax on tea.

3.4 - The Boston Tea Party

The tax levied on tea lead to a colonial boycott of tea imported by the British East India Company. (and some have speculated this may be the reason Americans today prefer coffee to tea). Instead, Americans were buying their tea on the black market. To purchase from the East India Company was to validate the tax on tea and thus Parliament's right to tax the colonies without representation. In 1773 the Tea Act was passed which gave the East India Company the right to import directly to the colonies without first going through England. In effect, this removed a financial burden on the trade and made the tea cheaper for the American customers. But they still refused to buy. The Tea Act was not a direct tax on the colonists but it represented British control over commodities being imported to the colonies. As such it was resisted.

Protests intensified around seven particular ships carrying tea to the colonies containing over half a million pounds worth of tea. In Charleston, Philadelphia and New York, the ships were turned away as those who would have purchased the shipment refused to do so. The ships took their cargo back to England. But in Boston, three ships were refused permission to leave by the colonies governor Thomas Hutchison. They remained trapped in Boston harbour for twenty days before an incident on the 16th December 1773. A group of 'Sons of Liberty' disguised themselves as Mohawk natives and managed to get aboard the ships, throwing their cargo overboard. The shipment was worth nine thousand pounds and was entirely lost.

Parliament retaliated against the state of Massachusetts Bay with the Coercive Acts in 1774, known to the Americans as the Intolerable Acts. These consisted of;

- The Boston Port Act, which sealed the port of Boston until such time as the spoiled goods were paid for.

- Massachusetts Government Act which put the governance of the colony under direct Crown control

- Administration of Justice Act which allowed for trials of Royal officials to be held elsewhere in the Empire if it was felt they would not receive a fair trial in Massachusetts. George Washington dubbed this Act the Murder Act as he believed it would give British officials complete impunity to act against American colonists and escape justice (as few colonists would have the resources to travel beyond the colony to give evidence, let alone to Britain).

In Massachusetts and beyond there was outrage at these measures. It demonstrated Britain's belief that they could undermine the colony's self-determination, removing any power from the colonists whenever they wanted. If it could be done to Massachusetts it could be done anywhere. The effect of the Coercive Acts was to bring together the colonists as never before.

3.5 - The Continental Congress

In September 1774, the First Continental Congress was held in Philadelphia. It was the first unified act of the thirteen colonies and was prompted by their shared dislike and distrust of Britain. Present were men whose names would become synonymous with the coming revolution; George Washington, John Adams, Samuel Adams and Patrick Henry. The outcome of the Congress was an appeal to George III for a repeal of the Coercive Acts, a boycott of all British goods and the raising of militia in the colonies in preparation for British retaliation.

That came in February 1775, when the British government declared Massachusetts a colony in rebellion. British troops were ordered to seize weapons and ammunition supposedly being stored by the 'rebels' at Concord. Warnings went ahead of the British troops to defend the armoury at Concord. In a famous action, Paul Revere rode ahead of the British troops, which were advancing along the Charles River to Lexington, on horseback. He succeeded in reaching Lexington ahead of the British troops to warn Samuel Adams and John Hancock. British soldiers arrived on April 19th to find Lexington held by a militia force against them.

The two sides engaged and the militia was driven off but continued to harass the British troops until they retreated back to Boston. These would be the first shots of the Revolutionary War. A second Continental Congress took place in May 1775. From this Congress came the formation of a Continental Army, under the command of George Washington and two documents to be sent to London. One was the 'Necessity for taking up arms' and the other the 'Olive Branch Petition'. The first outlined the grievances of the American colonists and why they had felt the need to take arms against Britain. The other asked for the request of the First Congress to be granted. It demonstrated that the representatives were prepared to fight for their rights but were not yet willing to completely remove themselves from rule by Britain. They wished to live under the Crown on equal terms to the rights they perceived to exist for those living in Britain itself. This would, however, soon change.

On June 17th, 1774 the first major battle of the revolution was fought outside Boston, the Battle of Bunker Hill. The militia was forced to retreat but inflicted losses on the British troops. This will have served to give confidence to the colonists. The British army was famed as a professional standing army, which was now facing in battle men who were farmers, clerks, in fact, any profession except soldier. Some of the militia may have fought in the French-Indian War but were not expected to be a match for the infamous British redcoats.

3.6 - Declaration of Independence

Despite the placatory documents produced by the Second Continental Congress, by 1776 there was a growing dissatisfaction with the idea of remaining part of a monarchical government. Enlightenment ideas were reaching the colonies from Europe, the same writings that would later inspire the French to revolution. Revolution was now being openly spoken of by men such as Patrick Henry, who uttered the famous words "Give me liberty or give me death." Most influential of all though was Thomas Paine. Paine had settled in America, from Britain, in 1774 and on the 10th January 1776 published a pamphlet entitled 'Common Sense' in Philadelphia. It became a runaway success, with 100,000 copies printed in the first two months and more than half a million before the end of the Revolution.

'Common Sense' described the failures of the monarchical system as a type of government. He went on to outline a plan for an ideal governmental system. The eventual structure of the independent American government, which would be formed by the Constitution mirrored Paine's model closely. He is known to history as one of the Fathers of the Revolution and his work would have been read or read to the majority of men who now took arms for their liberty.

In July 1776, the Second Continental Congress issued a Declaration of Independence. This declared the thirteen colonies independent from British rule. Thomas Jefferson drafted the declaration which was ratified by the Congress on the 4th July 1776. It re-christened the colonies as the 'United States of America'. It gave the reasons for the revolution, outlined the Americans grievances against the Crown but more importantly it made clear, in a preamble to the declaration the belief that '...all men are created equal.'. This concept alone was revolutionary and would just a decade later inspire the French people to orgies of violence in pursuit of their own unalienable rights. It rejected forever the idea of the United States being part of Great Britain as it claimed the existence of certain 'unalienable' rights. America could never accept the rule of a monarch who governed on the principle of the 'divine right of kings'.

3.7 - The Revolutionary War

Progress since the opening shots of the war at Lexington was mixed for the Americans. Victories at Fort Ticonderoga in 1774 were balanced by defeat at the Battle of Bunker Hill in June 1775, though the British lost more than a 1,000 men in their victory. Initially, the Americans suffered a series of defeats. The largest of these came on August 27th, 1776 at the Battle of Brooklyn Heights when Washington in command of approximately 18,000 American troops attempted to defend Manhattan island from a British force of 32,000 arriving by sea. The Americans were outflanked and forced to withdraw across Manhattan island pursued by the British. Ultimately, heavy rain and fog served to provide cover for a daring escape into Pennsylvania for Washington and his troops. The campaign cost him 300 men and more than a 1,000 lost as prisoners. Many of the American prisoners of war would have been held in the harbour of Manhattan aboard British warships. Conditions would have been difficult aboard these prison ships with disease rife. This added to the American casualties by the war's end.

Having suffered heavy losses attempting to defend New York and being forced to scramble away in defeat, the morale of the Continental Army was low and questions were being asked of its commander George Washington. Washington was able to restore the morale of his men with a stunning victory against the British army's Hessian mercenary forces on the 25th December 1776. Gambling that the Hessians would be celebrating Christmas and unprepared to fight he led the Continental Army across a frozen Delaware River in an attack on Trenton, New Jersey. They caught their enemy completely unprepared and achieved a much-needed victory. They also captured large quantities of weaponry and ammunition to bolster their own supplies.

Fighting continued into 1777 with few victories for the Americans until September 19th, when the Continental Army encountered a British force at Saratoga, New York. As had been a characteristic tactic throughout the war thus far, American woodsmen proved deadly as snipers. They attacked, invisibly, from wooded areas and proved deadly in their pursuit of British officers. Many British soldiers would later begin to desert under the pressure of marching through the hostile country-side under constant threat of sniper attacks from the trees.

After an initial victory, the Continental Army was forced to retreat when British reinforcements arrived under General Burgoyne. For over a month, Burgoyne waited for more troops with which to pursue the Americans. Meanwhile, the British troops were facing rationing as their supplies dropped. Eventually, Burgoyne attempted an attack against a superior American force and was heavily defeated. He retreated but was ultimately forced to surrender. It was the biggest American victory of the war so far and finally provided the British that the colonists were serious opponents. It made the same statement to the kingdom of France, persuading the French to ally themselves with the Americans. French involvement in the American revolutionary war would gain little for France. But it would bring the kingdom's finances to its knees and result in the uprising of the French peasant classes in the revolution. For now, the arrival of France and its allies would mean Britain was fighting a coalition of European rivals as well as the Continental Army of America.

The winter of 1777 saw the Continental Army resting at Valley Forge, Pennsylvania. The army was also low on supplies, forced to subsist on flour and water. Disease in camp was rife and cases of dysentery, typhoid and smallpox as well as the freezing conditions would claim the lives of 2,000 men by spring. In January of 1778, a representative of the Continental Congress arrived to inspect the army. The result was a much needed granting of supplies and guarantees of maintained supply lines from Congress by February. The turning point at their Valley Forge camp though was the arrival of Baron Friedrich Wilhelm von Stueben.

A veteran of the Prussian army he arrived from the French and was immediately made Inspector General of the Army by Washington. He began to personally deliver training to the Americans. He taught them movement between formations, how to load and fire their muskets in line and perform a bayonet charge. He also provided the American commanders with a training manual, which had to be translated from German, which remained the staple of US military training for the next forty years.

Another foreigner arrived at Valley Forge who would prove instrumental in the American victory. Marie Joseph Paul Yves Roch Gilbert Du Motier, otherwise known as the Marquis de Lafayette, was a French nobleman who became a commander of American forces and a close friend of George Washington. Upon returning to France he would end up commanding troops in the early years of the revolution there too. Lafayette was instrumental, along with the American minister to France, Benjamin Franklin, to securing a French alliance against Britain.

The end came in 1781 when American forces in the south forced British general Cornwallis to the Yorktown peninsula in Virginia. A French victory over the Royal Navy at the Battle of Chesapeake Bay meant that the French controlled the waters around Virginia, leaving Cornwallis trapped. Thus began the Siege of Yorktown. Under intense artillery bombardment from land and sea, the British troops attempted to escape across the York River. They hoped to make their way through American lines to the city of New York which was held by the British. However, as the weather had saved Washington on Manhattan, it now intervened again. A storm made the river uncrossable and Cornwallis was forced to request terms of surrender.

The official ceremony of surrender took place on the 19th of October 1781. Cornwallis was the commander of all British forces in America. His surrender signalled the defeat of the British. It also signalled the defeat of the government of British Prime Minister, Lord North. His government did not long survive the surrender at Yorktown and his successors were keen to bring about peace. Britain had been fighting not just in America but had faced a native rebellion in India and conflict with the Dutch and French in the Caribbean.

Peace talks began in Paris in 1782. The terms eventually offered by the British were generous, offering not only recognition of the United States as an independent country but seceding all territory east of the Mississippi, north of Florida and south of Quebec to the Americans. This increased the land of the original thirteen states significantly. The Treaty of Paris was signed on September 3rd, 1783 and the United States was born.

3.8 - Constitution

In May of 1787 representatives of the states gathered in Philadelphia to transform the Articles of Confederation that had been passed by the Second Continental Congress into a formal, federal constitution. The representatives became known as the Congress of Confederation. It would not prove an easy task as there were some significant differences in opinion over certain issues. One was how states would be represented, whether equally or according to the size of the population. Another was the issue of slavery, between slave-owning states and those in favour of abolition. The bicameral nature of the new government was a solution to the problem of representation; the Senate would represent each state equally, the House of Representatives would see representation weighted by population.

The issue of slavery was never addressed, merely postponed. It would be addressed a century later amid the carnage of the American Civil War, still one of the bloodiest conflicts the United States has ever engaged in.

To guarantee the freedom of states from an overpowering central government, such as they had experienced under the British, checks and balances were put in place to ensure no single arm of government could rule unopposed. Thus the executive, in the person of a president, had the power to enact or veto legislation, acting as a check on the legislature. The legislature, Congress, had the power to produce legislation but were checked by the President. The judiciary was independent of both and acted as a check on both, due to the appointment of Supreme Court judges for life.

Several of the states refused to accept the first draft of the constitution, resulting in ten amendments. These ten amendments became known as the Bill of Rights. This document guarantees the personal and unalienable rights of American citizens such as; freedom of speech, freedom of religion, the right to the due process of law and others. It was the ratification of these ten amendments that served to allay the fears of a United States government becoming a dictatorial power such as the British Crown. For the Congress and the people whom they represented this was the single biggest fear.

The final piece of the puzzle was the installation of an individual to serve as President. The election was held in 1789 and George Washington was chosen unanimously by every elector in the Electoral College, the only US president to achieve this. He set the tone for the office, refusing suggested titles such as 'Majesty' and 'Highness' in favour of 'Mr President'. He also rejected suggestions of royal dress and instead chose the clothes of a businessman. In this, he showed that the American President of this new nation was also one of the people and was not in any way elevated above them. These were truly revolutionary concepts in a world where, almost without exception, ruling elites presided over nation states and social hierarchies were rigid and unbreakable. The United States had fought to remove the barriers between rulers and ruled. It would take violence to do the same elsewhere in the world in the coming years.

3.9 – Summary

The American Revolution grew out of the desire to be treated fairly by the country which many American colonists came from and still admired. Regarded as a source of revenue by the British ruling elite rather than people deserving of equal rights to those enjoyed at home, the American colonists were pushed further and further away from Great Britain. Protests of increasing violence were not directed with hatred towards the British nation as an enemy but rather against the ideas that Americans could be forced to pay taxes without also be given the right to representation.

When the Continental Congress met it was to request of the British Crown a redress for this grievance; an end to taxations being levied against the colonies without the consent of those colonies. Even when the colony of Massachusetts was being declared in rebellion and British troops mobilised the Continental Congress was not yet ready to talk about independence. When the Declaration finally came it brought with it eight years of warfare among the territory of the thirteen colonies. This war was not restricted to battlefields between professional armies. The American Continental Army was a volunteer force recruited from among the ordinary men of the colonies.

An estimated 6 thousand of these citizen soldiers would be killed in action with another 17,000 dying of disease, either from injuries sustained or as prisoners of war. The British forces lost around 24,000 to battlefield deaths, disease and injuries while German mercenaries fighting with the British lost around 8,000 men. In all, approximately 50,000 may have died during the American revolutionary war.

But these are only the direct casualties. For though the Founding Fathers professed to believe in the equality of all men it is clear that they had a narrow view of who this applied to. Native Americans would not be recognised as citizens of the United States until 1866. Black men would not be able to vote until 1869, almost a hundred years after the Declaration of Independence with its 'self-evident' truths on the rights of man. Women would not be able to vote until the passage of the Nineteenth Amendment in 1920.

But it was the issue of slavery specifically which would go on to cause much suffering in the life of the United States. It would become a dividing issue between abolitionist Northern states with their manufacturing economy and urban culture and the agricultural South. The failure to address the issue at the Congress of Confederation merely stored the problem up for later generations and almost tore the new country apart. Even after the Civil War, racial inequality has been a major issue in the United States ever since.

Despite this, the purpose of the American Revolution was gain independence from imperialist Great Britain for the thirteen American colonies, and create a system of government that would guarantee the rights and civil liberties of the American people against tyranny. This, it achieved in spectacular fashion. It proved not only to be of benefit to the American people but also served as an example to others. Specifically, the French people could see the Americans rising up to overthrow the monarchy of Britain. The writings of men like Thomas Paine would serve as a revolutionary inspiration to the French. It can be no accident that when the Estates General of France met in 1789, the representatives of the Third Estate were so quick to assume control and act to guarantee the liberty of the working man and equality in their society. They had the example of the successful American revolution.

CHAPTER 4

THE GLORIOUS REVOLUTION

Introduction

The Glorious (or Bloodless) Revolution describes the overthrow of the Stuart dynasty which had ruled England, Wales Ireland and Scotland for almost ninety years beginning in the 1600's. James II of England (VII of Scotland) abandoned his throne in a moment of weakness and Parliament offered it to his son-in-law William Prince of Orange. It marked the overthrow of a Catholic monarch in a country that feared and despised Roman Catholics. It also marked the end of a period of constitutional crisis that had seen England and Wales torn apart by civil war and had resulted in the execution of James father, Charles I.

The names originate from the fact that in exchange for the throne of England, William and his wife agreed to the enacting of the Bill of Rights in 1689. This guaranteed the rights of Englishmen, the rights and powers of Parliament which became superior to those of the King. It was the end of absolute monarchy and the divine right of Kings, the beginning of the modern Parliamentary democracy that Britain possesses today. Though the events of this change of power were relatively bloodless they sparked a chain reaction which was anything but. The consequences of the Glorious Revolution in terms of relations between Protestants and Catholics, particularly in Northern Ireland, were catastrophic and would be felt to the present day.

4.1 - The Stuart Dynasty

To understand the events of the Glorious Revolution it is necessary to understand the backdrop for these events, England as it was at the end of the seventeenth century. In 1605 James Charles Stuart (James VI of Scotland) became king of England and Ireland, unifying the Scottish and English thrones. James was offered the throne of England to ensure a smooth succession following the death of Elizabeth I in 1603. James was a devout Protestant, from his reign came the much-celebrated translation of the Bible known as the King James Bible. His time as King also saw the defeat of a supposed Catholic plot to assassinate King and Parliament both. It was a time of fear and paranoia towards Catholics in England.

In 1597, whilst still only the King of Scotland, James wrote a treatise called 'The True Law of Free Monarchies'. In this work, he laid out the fundamental concept of the divine right of kings. Monarchs were selected by God, he reasoned and were therefore elevated above normal men. This view would lead him to a fractious relationship with the institution of Parliament, which saw itself as the voice of the people and an equal partner with the King. James would have an acrimonious relationship with Parliament during his reign and, following his death in 1625 so would his son and heir, Charles I, and his grandsons Charles and James.

Both James I and Charles I would make frequent use of the King's right to prorogue (send home the representatives of Parliament, not to meet again without royal permission) and to dissolve (disband Parliament until fresh elections are held) Parliaments. Both monarchs would exercise these powers whenever men in either the House of Commons or Lords spoke out to vociferously against the King. This, in turn, led to the rise of a radical group within the Commons who believed the King was attempting to silence the voice of the people and rule as an absolute monarch without Parliament. Eventually, this led to civil war, as radical Puritans seized control of Parliament and took to arms for the defence of their rights.

This raged from 1642 to 1651 and touched almost every corner of England and Wales, tearing apart families and communities. It would end with the execution of Charles I as an enemy of the people in 1649. This was followed by eleven years of dictatorship under the rule of Oliver Cromwell, leader of the Parliamentary forces during the war. The monarchy was restored in 1660 and the new king, Charles II (son of the deposed Charles I) ruled with the cooperation of Parliament for most of his reign.

4.2 - The Cavalier Parliament & The Clarendon Code

After Charles II accession to the throne in 1660, the Convention Parliament which had organised the restoration was dissolved and fresh elections held. In 1661 a new Parliament met which would be known as the Cavalier Parliament. They would remain in place until 1679. This was probably the most harmonious relationship any Stuart monarch had with a Parliament. They were made up of Royalists who were Anglican Protestant in their religious outlook. They did not want to return to an absolute ruler nor did they desire religious extremism such as had existed under the Puritan, Oliver Cromwell. Charles appeared to mirror their desires for a stable country with moderate policies and views.

However, in one area Parliament was prepared to legislate harshly to protect that stability. From 1661 to 1665 a series of acts were passed which came to be known as the 'Clarendon Code' after Charles principal advisor Edward Hyde, Earl of Clarendon. The Clarendon Code was designed to strengthen the Church of England and persecute any who advocated any differences with the Anglican Church. These included Puritans (who rejected the Anglican bishops and concepts such as communion), Catholics and Quakers, in fact, anyone who did not fit the tradition of high church Anglicanism. The Clarendon Code prohibited anyone from holding an office of state who had not taken Anglican Communion within the last twelve months, prohibited any religious assembly of more than five people except within the Church of England.

The Clarendon Code represented a formalising of the anti-Catholic feeling that had characterised the political elite of England for almost a century. Catholicism was perceived as a great world evil. One of the reasons for this was the loyalty which all Catholics were commanded to give to the Pope. This was seen in England as a loyalty that would always be above and beyond any loyalty to the King or the people of England. The example of Catholic monarchs in Europe, such as Louis XIV, was that they were dictators who ruled with no elected assembly and no democratic voice given to the people. For the English this was anathema.

4.3 - The Exclusion Crisis

In the 1660's England fought a disastrous war against their mercantile rival, Holland. It resulted in the resignation from the post of lord admiral of the king's brother James, Duke of York. The resignation came amid accusations of corruption at the highest level and embezzlement of funds. James was not popular with the public as a result. This would have consequences when his own reign began. The scandal resulted in the resignation of the king's closest advisor, and engineer of his restoration, the Earl of Clarendon. In his place, a group of ministers, collectively known as the 'Cabal', became advisors to the crown.

Their ascent signalled the beginning of a split between Commons and Lords in Parliament. Until this point, the House of Commons had been effectively subservient to the Lords but dislike and distrust of the Cabal led to a power shift. Sir William Coventry formed what was effectively the first political party within the Commons, known as the 'Country Party' for his vocal opposition to the Crown and the Cabal. Opposed to the Country Party were the Court Party who were royalists.

The political infighting between the Commons and Lords, and within the Commons themselves tried the patience of the Cabal such that they recommended to the King the prorogation of Parliament. It was a mistake both his father and grandfather had made before him. Each had tried to silence vocal opposition within Parliament only to recall it when in need of money (as only Parliament could authorise tax collection or the raising of new taxes. Each time Parliament returned, it was more hostile than it had been before. The Third Anglo-Dutch War, which began in 1672 in alliance with France against Holland, was the reason for Charles recalling Parliament in 1675. But instead of granting Charles the funds he needed to prosecute the war, they were more concerned with the Declaration of Indulgence decree he had issued in their absence. The Declaration of Indulgence served to abolish penal laws against Catholics and Anglican dissenters. It had been recommended by the Cabal and was in line with Charles own moderate views on religion.

Parliament was incensed that the King had revoked an Act of Parliament without their consent. He was forced to reverse this act and agree to the passage of the Test Act in 1673. This was a statement of the power of Parliament, an attack on his advisors and a cementing of the anti-Catholic bias which dominated English society. The Test Act required office holders to publicly reject Catholicism and accept Anglican communion. Many of Charles ministers could not stomach it and resigned. By now public and Parliamentary sentiment, at one time ferociously anti-Dutch, had now swung in favour of Holland. One reason for this was the tales of charismatic, brave young prince, William of Orange.

William had been named stadtholder (elected leader) of the United Provinces of the Netherlands in 1672 following a disastrous war fought against France and England which had brought the Dutch Republic to its knees. William refused to surrender however and would ultimately liberate his country. William was the nephew of Charles I (his mother Mary was Charles daughter) and was a cousin to both Charles II and James, Duke of York. In his defeat of the French, the anti-Catholic masses in England (and in particular London) now had stories of the brave and most importantly Protestant hero of Holland. This would have fed into their resistance to England continuing any alliance with France or any further wars with Holland. It also laid the groundwork for William's eventual accession to the throne.

In a further demonstration of the power of Parliament, Charles was manoeuvred into marrying off his niece Mary (daughter of his brother James, Duke of York) to William. In exchange, Parliament granted the funds Charles wanted. The King could now join Holland in alliance against France. Unfortunately, while the marriage went ahead, the war did not. France and Holland reached a peace treaty in 1677. The character of Parliament had changed markedly since the Convention Parliament which had restored Charles to the throne. They had been welcoming of the monarchy and keen to encourage cooperation. Now the issue of Catholicism was driving a wedge between King and Parliament which would come to head with Parliament's desire to prevent the King's brother James becoming King.

This intervention, known as the Exclusion Crisis, was precipitated by the so-called Popish Plot. This was a fiction created by a man named Titus Oates. Its purpose was to stir up hatred against Catholics. Oates created a fictional plot by the Catholic church to assassinate the King and brought it to the attention of the authorities in 1678, complete with documentary evidence and the names of the conspirators. An investigation began and he was interviewed by the King's closest advisors as well as the Privy Council. Nothing came of his revelations, the King, in particular, was not convinced, until the murder of Sir Edmund Berry Godfrey on the 12th of October

1678. It was blamed on the Catholic conspiracy and Oates named numerous men who he claimed were part of the plot. Parliament passed the Second Test Act in December 1878 amid a furore of anti-Catholic hatred among the people. This banned Catholics from holding seats in either of the Houses of Parliament. One of the leaders of the Country party in the lords, the Earl of Shaftesbury attempted to have the king's brother James excluded from the line of succession (James was a Catholic).

Shaftesbury's actions prompted the Exclusion Crisis which ran from 1679 to 1691. It led to the formation of the Whig party who wished James struck off the line of succession and the Tory party who were pro-royalist. The Whigs were defeated in their attempts to exclude James but the precedence had now been set. Anti-Catholic hysteria gripped the nation, going beyond the rhetoric of politicians. Effigies of the pope were burnt in the streets. London, in particular, was a city proud of its Protestantism. The concept of being English was now inextricably tied with the Protestant faith. It is important to remember that at this point there was no question of the right of King Charles II to his throne. There was no speculation of removing the King and returning to the state of a republic, as had been done under Oliver Cromwell. But there was serious concern over the succession. Charles had no legitimate heir. This meant that the next in line to the throne was his brother James.

4.4 - King James II

Charles, I died in February 1685 after suffering a stroke. He had no legitimate children and so James, Duke of York was his heir. James had been raised a Protestant but by the 1670's was leaning towards Catholicism and seemed to have openly embraced the faith by 1673 when he married Mary of Modena, a Catholic, Italian princess. It seemed certain that in a Catholic household such as James and Mary had now formed, any children would also be raised Catholic. Charles had intervened when James and his first wife had shown a preference for Catholicism, insisting that their two daughters (Mary and Anne, both future Queen of England) be raised under the Anglican faith. The threat of a Catholic dynasty would become very real if James and Mary produced a child who survived infancy.

Such were the fears in Parliament and among the people of London (whose ability to be mobilised into a mob had been a powerful tool against the Kings of England since the reign of Charles I). But James seems to have been blind to this. He appointed an inner council of advisors, all Catholics. He summoned a brand new Parliament and ensured that his supporters outweighed his opponents in its representatives. Universities were forced to accept Catholic students and Catholics were appointed to important positions within the institutions themselves. James created a Commission for Ecclesiastical Causes in 1686, which was a revival of the Court of High Commission which had been abolished by Parliament during the reign of his father, Charles I. In effect, this body took charge of the Church of England and was intended to seek out and punish any who opposed the King.

Upon his ascension, to the throne, James faced two armed rebellions against his rule. In South-West England, the Duke of Monmouth, James Scott, the illegitimate son of Charles II declared himself the true heir to the throne. He was supported by an attempted rising in Scotland orchestrated by the Earl of Argyll. Both were defeated but in the aftermath, James chose not to disband the army which had been raised to fight the rebellions. This was against the historical convention that armies were not maintained in peacetime. This action from any English King would have caused an outcry of protest but from a King who was openly Catholic and proceeding to fill the offices of state with Catholics, this action would have seemed to presage a Catholic autocracy. To make matters worse, the maintenance of a peacetime standing army was a policy also followed by Louis XIV of France, the ultimate Catholic dictator.

4.5 - The Trial of the Seven Bishops

On April 18th, 1688 James used his royal prerogative to pass the Declaration of Indulgence, which his brother had also tried to pass into law. This reversed the proscriptions against non-Anglican religions and reversed the Test Acts. On May 4th, 1688 The Declaration was ordered to be read out to every church congregation from the pulpit. The protest against this reversal of the laws against Catholics and other religious minorities centred on seven bishops, leader by the Bishop of Canterbury who signed a petition against it. The petition was presented to the King on the 18th May and was furiously rejected. It was subsequently printed and distributed to the people of London. The King believed it to be a statement of rebellion and ordered the seven arrested for the distribution of the petition on a charge of seditious libel.

The trial took place on the 29th June 1688. During the trial, the bishops refused to repudiate the petition but also refused to admit any wrongdoing in its distribution. They became the focal point for the massed protest of London, the voice of the dissenters. Every day crowds gathered around Whitehall to see the bishops taken into court. Men and women crowded around, to touch them, hoping for a blessing. They became heroes, fighting for the freedom of true Englishmen against a Catholic monarch who wanted to be a dictator. On the 30th June, after a night of deliberation, the bishops were found not guilty by a jury.

4.6 - The last straw

To the Catholic fearing people of England the reign of the new King had brought, Catholic elevation to the highest offices of state, the maintenance of a standing army loyal to their Catholic king and an attempt to use royal prerogative to repeal laws passed by Parliament. King James II had, in the eyes of many, showing that his desire was to rule as a Catholic, surrounded by men of his own faith and with an army to ensure that his will is made manifest, regardless of the wishes of the people. He seemed to be emulating Louis XIV, a despised despot. On the 10th June 1688, as the protest was rife against the Declaration of Indulgence, Queen Mary gave birth to a son. He would be named James Francis and he would be raised as a Catholic. The birth of a son displaced James eldest daughter Mary (wife of William of Orange) from her position as heir to the throne and raised the prospect of a Catholic dynasty.

It also forced both sides into positions they could not reverse. James must continue with his policy of restoring Catholicism to England, for the sake of his son and his son's inheritance. The previously warring Whig and Tory parties, now united against James' religion had to act to prevent a Catholic dynasty.

It was not only the English political elite and London masses that found themselves concerned over James' religion and the direction he may intend to take England. In the United Provinces of the Netherlands, William of Orange was also concerned. He harboured in Amsterdam those who had fled England as James' opponents. This had at one time included the Duke of Monmouth, who had gone on to make an attempt for James' throne. Now, English and Scottish dissenters began to gather around William again.

William was driven by one motivation, the desire to see his country safe from the might of France. In 1672 England and France had been allies and had brought the United Provinces to their knees. William's own marriage to the English royal family had been driven by the need to deprive Louis XIV of his English ally in future. But with a Catholic on the throne of England, it seemed that family connections or no, France was now a natural ally of the English. William too saw his options narrowing. James could not be trusted to rule for a few years then quietly die and leave England to his daughter. Mary had been displaced and England would be Catholic for another generation at least.

4.7 - William acts

William of Orange was not a King. He did not have the luxury of unilateral that James of England or Louis of France possessed. The office of stadtholder which William possessed was that of a civil servant, given the duty of maintaining law, order and peace within the Dutch Republic. But he was answerable to the provinces which made up the Republic. He could not simply raise an army and a fleet to invade England. William's action came in April 1688, when he made clear to two of James' English opponents that if he (William) were to be invited to come to England by men of the 'best interest and most value' in order to 'rescue the nation' he would come, and would be ready by the end of September. William gave this information to Edward Russell and Admiral Arthur Herbert, both opponents of James' policies.

In return, William was given a list of names, each assigned a code. When the 'Seven Bishops' were acquitted Admiral Herbert travelled back to Holland in disguise and handed William a list of seven numbers. From these numbers and the earlier document he had been given William knew who the men of 'interest and value' were that had requested him to 'rescue the nation'. William had been denied permission to expand the Dutch Navy before, by the powerful mercantile interests of Amsterdam, who feared war with their best export customer, France. Louis XIV himself provided William with the answer there. Louis, against the advice of his ambassador to the Netherlands, began a trade war with the Dutch which in turn caused a financial panic. This turned many Dutch merchants against France. Louis' ambassador, D'Avaux reported a massive military buildup by William, intended for England. But Louis refused to believe it and instead of making a show of force against Holland which would have led the Dutch States-General to refuse William permission to take Dutch troops away from home, Louis instead committed himself to a military venture in the south.

With their French markets denied to them and no immediate military threat from France, the States-General gave William permission to take his troops across the North Sea to England. On the 10th October 1688, William made an open declaration of his intent to invade England. It stated that William's actions were driven by the desire to defend the 'Laws, liberties and customs' which were being 'openly transgressed and annulled'. This was not a conquest as the Romans and the Normans had done centuries before, and the Spanish attempted. This was an invasion intended to liberate the English people from their tyrannical King.

4.8 - The 'liberation' of England

William and his fleet landed at Torbay in Devon on the 5th November 1688. His force numbered some fourteen thousand men with almost four thousand cavalry and sixteen artillery pieces. They were recruited from all over northern Europe, including Germans, Finns, Poles and Dutch as well as a number of Scots. They were a well-armed, well-supplied body of professional soldiery who had cut their teeth against the might of France. The fleet which carried them was the largest England had ever faced, dwarfing the infamous 'Spanish Armada' of the sixteenth century.

King James controversial 'standing army' was stationed at Salisbury Plain but was weakening fast. By the time James, as their commander in chief reached them on the 19th of November he was reported to be suffering acutely from stress. First, his much-prized cavalry deserted, then James' son-in-law (Prince George of Denmark). This prompted James to flee back to London, leaving his army to further desertions. Desperate, James sent away his wife and heir to France, following them on the 11th December. Upon crossing the Thames, James threw the Great Seal of England into the river. This was the imprint which all laws in England were made under and without which no government was possible. James was fleeing his throne and his country and trying to ensure a state of chaos left behind him.

His departure was followed by widespread unrest as anti-Catholic mobs rampaged through the streets of towns and cities, attacking anything that seemed to them to represent Catholicism. This was fuelled by rumour and conspiracy theories principally a tale that London was to be imminently attacked by an Irish army intent on massacring the Protestant population. The news of the King's flight, it seemed, had precipitated a mass panic. The political elite of England was ready for the order to be restored, and with James' departure, only Prince William could do that. James himself would not be successful in his escape attempt. He would be captured by two fishermen and imprisoned. On the 23rd December 1688, William would allow him to leave for France and James would never return to England again.

4.9 - The 'bloodless' revolution

With James gone a decision was made by the House of Lords to declare that the King's desertion of his country represented an abdication of the throne. James had laid the groundwork for this by issuing writs for a new Parliament to be elected after receiving news of William's landing in Torbay. He had allowed for a new government to be formed in a desire to try and bring Parliament back to his side. Now, that new Parliament would strip him of his royal title and formally offer the throne to William and Mary (Mary being a legitimate heir) as joint rulers. It was decided that the Lords should administer to the governance of the nation while the joint monarchs took charge of the army. On the 29th December 1688, William and Mary took their place in the new administration.

In February 1689 Parliament created a document that would be known as the 'Declaration of Rights'. This would later be amended and become the 'Bill of Rights'. This outlined the powers of Parliament and the prospective monarchs (they had not yet been formally crowned but were merely part of the temporary government structure). The 'Bill of Rights' would form the cornerstone of the 'Glorious Revolution'. It made provisions for regular Parliaments and forbade the monarch from influencing the selection of members. Monarchs would be forbidden from embarking on a military venture without the permission of Parliament and were forbidden from maintaining a standing army.

The freedoms of the ordinary people were also protected. Freedom of speech was guaranteed as was freedom of religion. Monarchs would not be allowed to determine the religion of their subjects while Parliament passed a 'Toleration Act' which undid the compulsion to join the Church of England and undid the Catholic persecution that had been practised by opponents to the King. Most importantly, the concept of the 'divine right of kings' which was proposed by James VI of Scotland in the late sixteenth century and practised by his sons and grandsons, was formally abolished. The monarchy of England, Ireland, Wales & Scotland was now on the road to becoming the constitutional monarchy of Great Britain. The foundations of the modern British Parliament had been laid.

4.10 - Aftermath

William and Mary were crowned jointly on April the 11th 1689 but their coronation would not be unchallenged. A month earlier, on the 12th March, James landed in Ireland to join an army that had been raised for him there. There had been fighting in Ireland since William's landing in England in November 1688. James had appointed Richard Talbot, First Earl of Tyrconnell as his Lord Deputy of Ireland. Talbot set about suppressing any opposition to James in Ireland. This was mainly concentrated in the north where the majority of English and Scottish immigrants to Ireland had settled.

James landed in Ireland with six thousand French troops at Kinsale and marched to Dublin where he presided over a Parliament in which he promised the return of lands in Ireland and England, taken from Catholics during the rule of Oliver Cromwell. James was also forced to pass a decree stating that England had no right to pass laws over Ireland. With such legislation being enacted any chance James might have had of being restored to the throne disappeared. Such terms would have been unacceptable, even to English Catholics. War now descended on Ireland. Protestant guerrilla groups were formed and were highly effective against James' army commanded by Talbot.

William landed at Carrickfergus on the 14th June 1690 and pursued James' force south. They met on the river Boyne on the 12th July. It was a victory for William though not a decisive one. But it was enough to persuade James to abandon his campaign. He returned to France, leaving his army behind. William offered surrender terms to the soldiers of James' army but not to the landed gentry who had supported him. Because of these harsh terms, the Irish gentry fought on.

They were eventually defeated on the 23rd September 1691 after a series of bloody battles and sieges that left more than eight thousand of the Jacobites (the name given to the followers of James) dead. The Treaty of Limerick in October 1691 offered pardons to any Catholics who swore fealty to William and Mary. However, this was undone completely by the Irish Parliament in 1697 which refused to recognize the treaty and introduced harsh penal laws which discriminated against Catholics.

The result of the 'Glorious Revolution' in England justifies the name entirely. A Catholic, the potential despot, was dethroned and a constitutional monarchy created in an entirely bloodless revolution. The stage was set for the emergence of Parliament as the voice of the people to serve as the true government of England. From these beginnings, England would become Great Britain and a true democracy. In Ireland, however, the revolution cannot be claimed to be either bloodless or glorious. Thousands died in battle or from disease as Catholics fought Protestants for control of the thrones of the Three Kingdoms (Ireland, Scotland and England). While a settlement was reached in the Treaty of Limerick which may have forestalled future bloodletting, the Protestant landowners who controlled Parliament would not allow it to happen. Following the overturning of the Treaty of Limerick, the Protestant Ascendancy (the Protestant ruling class) ruled Ireland, relegating Catholics to an underclass.

This oppression of the Catholics would explode into bloody revolution in the twentieth century and a guerilla war between the British, Irish Republicans and Irish Unionists would claim the lives of thousands more until the 1990's. The 'Glorious Revolution' gave emancipation from oppression to one side and disenfranchisement to the other. It gave some people freedoms they had never before enjoyed, but those freedoms were not universal.

CHAPTER 5

THE RUSSIAN REVOLUTION

Introduction

The revolution of the Russian proletariat to overthrow the rule of the Tsars is arguably one of the most important and influential events of the twentieth century. It led to the birth of Communism and Socialism. When the Nazi regime arose in Germany, and the world was dragged into a second global conflict, the communist nature of the Soviet state guaranteed that the 'sleeping bear' of Russia would not remain neutral or become an ally of the Nazis. Hitler appears to have felt as much antipathy towards communists as he did towards the Jewish people. The inevitable attack on the Soviet Union doomed the Nazi domination of Europe, which had been a very real possibility until that point. It also led the way to a polarisation of world politics for fifty years in the post-war era as Communist Russia faced the United States. The Cold War led to a technology race the like of which the world has not seen either before or since, as the United States and the Soviet Union vied with each other to prove their respective political and economic models were the best. This brought the world to the brink of nuclear Armageddon but also fuelled the emergence of rocket and satellite technology without which the twenty-first century would be markedly different.

The constant drive to maintain weapons technologies capable of deterrence led to technological offshoots and breakthroughs that have transformed human society (such as computing). Even after the fall of the Soviet Union, it's legacy means that Russia remains a global power, with a formidable nuclear arsenal, powerful economy and huge resources. This is a relic of its status as a superpower during the Cold War, a position owed to the October Revolution.

And yet the Russian Revolution is doubtless one of the bloodiest and most brutal uprisings in human history. The repression of the Czarist regime was total and responsible for many atrocities against ordinary Russians. In the early years of the twentieth century the Bolshevik movement, born out of Marxism, was not a peaceful one. Under the leadership of men like Vladimir Lenin and Josef Stalin, the Bolsheviks organised themselves into armed groups which considered armed robbery and protection rackets to be acceptable means of fundraising. When the revolution happened it was as brutal and cruel as the overthrow of the French aristocracy and royal family in 1789 or the massacre of whites in the Haitian slave revolt. Not only did it see the Russian royal family indiscriminately slaughtered by vengeful bolsheviks but it led to the rise of one of the most violent and repressive political regimes that had ever existed.

When the communist regime was finally in place under the dominance of Josef Stalin millions would end up being sacrificed upon the altar of the Soviet supremacy. Pogroms (campaigns of persecution) were still carried out against the Jewish minority as they had been during the reign of the Czars. Freedom of speech was arguably more restricted under the communist regime because of the need of that form of government to totally control all aspects of social and economic life.

5.1 - Life under the Czars

To understand the Russian revolution we need to look at the circumstances which produced it. By 1917 Russia had been ruled by a monarchy, the Czars, for more than four hundred years. The ruling Romanov dynasty had ascended to the throne in 1613 and secured its position through corruption and intrigue. Russia was a feudal kingdom. The ruling elite lived a life of decadent luxury while the peasants worked the land for their benefit. The Romanovs, in particular, lived in spectacular luxury while the majority of their subjects lived in abject poverty. Unlike the European democracies, in Russia, the peasantry was effectively the property of the landowners. Russian 'serfs' could be bought and sold, their movements and their marriages heavily restricted.

This system of serfdom came to an end in 1861 under the rule of Czar Alexander II who feared revolution if concessions were not made. These reforms did little for the lives of most ordinary Russians however. Land was too expensive for them to purchase so they remained under the control of their landlords. One change that did result was that after two years they were able to move off their landlord's lands. This lead to a population movement away from rural areas and into the larger towns and cities. The Russian economy began to change as factories and mines grew with this influx of new workers. In turn, this growth saw more people flock to the cities to take jobs in factories and other new industries.

Life was no easier for the new urban workers. Conditions in factories and mines were dangerous and uncomfortable. Wages were low or often non-existent, with workers being paid in vouchers that were only redeemable at the company store. The main beneficiaries whether the peasants laboured in the fields or the factories was the landed, wealthy elite. This grossly unequal system was to explode into a violent uprising that would tear down the old regime and institute a new supposedly utopian society. The philosophy behind the revolt came from one man, Karl Marx.

5.2 - Marx

Karl Marx was born on the 5th May 1818 in Trier, Germany. Born into a middle-class family he studied economics and philosophy, then as an adult, he travelled widely across Europe. Born to parents inspired by Enlightenment philosophers, he grew up in a background of liberal thinking and modern ideas that would help shape his own. He followed an academic path to being a philosopher in the late 1830's, studying at the University of Berlin. But his doctoral thesis, which held that theology must always be inferior to philosophy, was considered too controversial for Berlin. In fact, Marx, and his contemporaries were proving too radical in their philosophical and sociological outlook for the conservative German universities. By 1842, Marx had left Berlin and academia to pursue a career in journalism. It was writing for the Rhineland News that he began to express an interest in economics and socialism.

The Rhineland News ended up being banned by the Prussian censor after a complaint by Russian monarch, Tsar Nicholas II. Marx bemoaned the degree to which the authorities controlled his output through the paper and moved on to Paris in 1843. There he worked for a paper called German-French Annals, which was an attempt to bring together German and French radical voices. For this publication, Marx wrote a piece entitled 'On the Jewish Question' which was the first time he explored the concept of the working classes as a revolutionary force. It would signify the first embrace of communism.

This paper collapsed, again due to pressure from the Prussian censor, and Marx would move on again. A significant turning point in his life came when he met Friedrich Engels on the 28th August 1844. The two would become lifelong friends and their meeting would signify a turning point in Marx' career. It was Engels who introduced Marx to his own work 'The Condition of the Working Class in England in 1844' which convinced Marx that the proletariat would be the instigators of the final revolution in history. Marx had at this point been studying political economics and just a few months after meeting Engels all of the relevant component pieces of Marx's socialist philosophy would be in place. From this philosophy would come his greatest and most influential works, namely; 'Capital' and 'The Communist Manifesto'

These works would be the foundation for the socio-economic system of 'Socialism' and 'Communism' both of which would be inspirations for the leaders of the Russian revolution. In the 'Communist Manifesto,' Marx argues that throughout human history societies have evolved whereby the majority of the population (the proletariat) live under the oppression of a property-owning elite (the bourgeoisie). The work goes on to predict that these societies are fundamentally unstable because of their oppressive nature, and the majority formed by the 'proletariat', and are doomed to descend into class warfare resulting in the overthrow of the 'bourgeoisie' by the 'proletariat'.

The 'Manifesto' claims that once the old system has been overthrown it will lead to the creation of a classless society in which each contributes according to their ability and receives according to their needs. This work was highly influential, especially with the man who would become a leader of the Russian Revolution, Vladimir Lenin. The 'Manifesto' was written as a plan of action for a political party which Marx had been associated with since his time as a journalist in Germany. They were known as the 'League of the Just' and operated as a secret, underground, organisation. Marx had come to realise that they were well placed to help bring about a mass uprising of European proletariat if they began operating openly as a political party. Consequently the 'Communist League' was born. The Marx-Engels authored pamphlet 'The Communist Manifesto' was the manifesto for that party.

5.3 - The Fall of the Romanovs

The last Czar of the Romanov dynasty was Nicholas II. He ascended the throne following the death of his father on the 1st November 1894. The country he inherited was already bubbling with revolutionary fervour. Nicholas' grandfather, Czar Alexander II had been assassinated by a radical workers group demanding social reform. Alexander III (Nicholas' father) had succeeded him and refused to grant permission for the formation of an elected assembly to represent the people. Under his reign, the Imperial boot of the autocratic Czar's pressed down harder than ever before. This included a series of laws aimed at the persecution of Russia's Jewish population.

Nicholas reign was also characterised by bloodshed, though he was more willing to accept reform than his father had been. Following his marriage in 1896, a feast was held which was to be shared with all the people of Moscow. A rumour spread that there was a shortage of food, resulting in a stampede of approximately one hundred thousand Muscovites. Around two thousand people were trampled to death in the panic. Mere hours after the disaster, Nicholas was seen attending a banquet held by his French allies, further harming his public image. Nicholas would come to known as Nicholas the Bloody in the aftermath of this event.

It was not an auspicious start for Nicholas, though he had done nothing directly. Then in January 1905, striking workers from Petrograd marched on the Czar's Winter Palace to present to him personally a petition outlining their grievances. Unfortunately, Nicholas was not present and the minister responsible for the palace ordered police to open fire on the protestors. The subsequent massacre came to be known as 'Bloody Sunday' and an estimated one thousand men, women and children were killed. It led to a series of strikes and revolts across Russia, including amongst regiments of the army and the crew of the battleship 'Potemkin'. This became known as the 'Revolution of 1905' and it forced Nicholas to institute a series of social reforms. These were published as the 'October Manifesto' on the 30th October 1905. It promised the institution of a constitution and the formation of an elected assembly to represent the people. This assembly would be known as the 'Duma'.

The 'Duma' met five times between 1905 and 1907 but each meeting was dissolved by Nicholas with no agreement reached. Meanwhile, the reasons for resentment against the Czar continued to mount. Grigori Rasputin, an enigmatic Siberian mystic, became a close advisor to the Romanovs but was despised by the people because of the rumours of occult practices. However, after he saved the life of her son, the Czarina was a staunch supporter of Rasputin and would not allow him to be dismissed. Then in 1914, Russia was drawn into the First World War. Russia suffered terrible losses during the war while the economic burden also took its toll. By 1917 there were food shortages as a result of so much of the Russian economy being converted to the war effort.

On the 8th of March 1817, protesters took to the streets in Petrograd to demand food. They were joined by a large number of striking industrial workers. Soldiers fired on the crowd who still refused to disperse. By the 12th of March, the soldiers had defected to join protesters. This was followed by the creation of a provisional government, headed by Alexander Kerensky, by the Duma on March 15th. The Petrograd Soviet seized control of the Russian army. Nicholas II abdicated his throne in favour of his brother Michael, who refused it. Power now fell to the Provisional government and the Petrograd Soviet (the city council of Petrograd, then the Russian capital). The reign of the Romanovs was over, the Czar had been overthrown.

5.4 - Lenin

The Provisional government, under Kerensky, was not popular with the Russian people. They advocated a continuation of Russian involvement in the War. This was against the popular view. It was also contrary to the wishes of the Russian army who had hoped for a withdrawal of Russian forces. The Provisional Government didn't address the issues which had caused the Russian people to revolt in the first place. There was no relief to the poor working conditions which many experienced in the factories. There was no relief to food shortages which led to food riots. Meanwhile, the Bolshevik party (literally meaning majority these represented the majority group in the Russian socialist movement that emerged in the 1900's) were seeking to politicize and radicalise the discontented industrial workers and rural peasantry. The Bolsheviks had emerged from the Russian Socialist Liberation Party that had driven the Czar from power. By 1917 the party had become split between those who wanted a further Communist revolution (the Bolsheviks) and those who supported Kerensky's policies. By October, Kerensky himself would be overthrown.

A new leader emerged to take his place, Vladimir Ilich Ulyanov, who would be better known by the surname he later chose for himself, Lenin. Lenin had been radicalised after the arrest of his brother for being part of the assassination of Czar Alexander III. Lening had gone to Kazan University and became a senior figure in an illegal political group. Upon graduation, he had become a writer and political agitator and had been arrested more than once, as well as spending time in a political prison in Siberia. Upon his release he travelled Europe, visiting with socialist politicians and political parties and writing many books and pamphlets on the subject of socialism. He had been a vocal opponent of Russia's involvement in the First World War. When Czar Nicholas abdicated in 1917, Lenin decided to return to Russia from Germany.

In his absence from Russia, the Bolsheviks had taken control of the Petrograd and Moscow Soviets following a failed coup attempt against Kerensky's Provisional Government. The Bolsheviks shared Lenin's Socialist views which were inspired by Marx. Lenin addressed a meeting of the Bolshevik Central Committee on the 10th October 1917 and argued for an armed insurrection to overthrow the Provisional government. The Committee voted for his action and later that month Bolsheviks seized key transport and communications sites in Petrograd. They besieged the Winter Palace and were famously helped by the crew of the battleship Aurora which opened fire on the palace.

The Provisional Government was overthrown and in its place, Lenin accepted the leadership of the 'Council of People's Commissars'. The 'Russian Social Democratic Labor' party was renamed the 'Russian Communist Party'. The government in Russia now rested with the 'Council of People's Commissars' which was led by Lenin, the 'Executive Committee' and the 'All-Russian Congress of Soviets' which elected the 'Executive Committee'. Between 1918 and 1918, however, the other branches of governments became more and more marginalised in favour of the 'Council of People's Commissars' while members of Russia's other political parties were expelled from office, turning Russia into a one-party state.

The Communist Party itself comprised a 'Politburo' (Political Bureau) an 'Orgburo' (and Organisational Bureau) and a 'Central Committee'. Lenin chaired the 'Council of Commissars' and held seats on both the 'Politburo' and the 'Central Committee' making him one of the most important members of the government. When an attempt was made on Lenin's life in January 1918, the Communist Party leadership decided to relocate to the Kremlin, in Moscow.

Lenin's regime began dismantling the old Russian state. Lands owned by Russian aristocracy or clergy were turned over to the people, the press was 'temporarily' gagged because many opposition voices in the press were deemed to be counter-revolutionary. In November 1917, Lenin issued the 'Declaration of the Rights of the of the Peoples of the Russias' this gave the right to any non-Russian ethnic groups living inside Russia to secede from Russia as independent states. Thus Finland, Poland, the Ukraine, Latvia, Lithuania and Estonia all gained their independence. Bolshevik parties were established in all of these new states and within a year the Russian republic had transformed into the 'Russian Soviet Federative Socialist Republic' which would become known to the outside wide as the 'USSR'.

Under Lenin's leadership, a system of nationalisations would take place to begin to transform Russian society into a Socialist society. All major industry was nationalised, with trades unions controlling factories, reporting to the 'Supreme Council of the National Economy'. All Russian banks were brought under state control as was the nation's gold supply. Foreign trade, utilities and transport were all nationalised as part of a centralised national economic plan. As well as this there was a mass education program, a system of free secondary education and separation of church and state (with religious education banned from schools).

With the 'Treaty of Brest-Litovsk on the 3rd March 1918, the new Russian state bowed out of the First World War, though surrendering a large amount of rich agricultural land to Germany as part of the negotiation. This did nothing to aid hungry peasants who were already short of food. Over the course of 1918, there was a series of devastating food riots. Lenin blamed the shortage on 'kulaks' which was the name given to wealthier peasants who, he alleged were hoarding grain in order to manipulate the price. This discontent would soon feed into a counter-revolutionary civil war between the Bolshevik 'Red' army and the Counter-Revolutionary 'White'. Lenin gave Leon Trotsky responsibility for the formation of the ed.

Trotsky was Lenin's effective second in command. He was a member of the 'Politburo' and had the title 'Commissar for Foreign Affairs'. Following the overthrow of the Provisional Government, Trotsky had been responsible for the formation of the Red Army into an effective fighting force and military arm of the Communist Party. He favoured brutal methods to conscript people into the Red Army and then force them to fight, including the taking of hostages from among family and friends.

The White armies opposing the Bolsheviks suffered the disadvantage of geographical separation. They were spread around the fringes of Russia, while the Red Army was concentrated around Moscow and Petrograd. Trotsky allowed officers who had previously served in the Czarist Russian army to take posts in the Red Army and they were able to defeat the White Army along all fronts. This victory was aided by the removal of the figureheads of the counter-revolutionary movement, the Romanov royal family. This was done in July 1918 when Czar Nicholas, his wife, three daughters and son were shot and bayoneted to death. The act was made public to demonstrate the total victory of the revolution and the futility of the White cause.

Lenin's regime fell short of full communism, fearing that this would not be accepted by the Russian people. He allowed small businesses and agriculture to remain in private hands. The policies that were re-organising the Russian economy were known as the 'New Economic Policy' and allowed the economy to recover from the ravages of war quickly. Lenin enjoyed a position of a benevolent dictator over the new Soviet people, and his control of the press reinforced the image of 'Papa Lenin' to such an extent that following his death in 1924 his body was mummified in order to be displayed to the public.

Lenin had presided over the revolution that had destroyed the Russian royal family, aristocracy and Church. He created a socialist state and built the infrastructure of the coming Communist regime. He approved brutal violence in repression of opposition but this would pale in comparison to the man who would succeed him.

5.5 - Stalin

Josef Stalin rose to power as one of Lenin's lieutenants. He was born in Georgia on 18th December 1878. Stalin experienced a difficult upbringing. His father was a cobbler who was driven out of business by failing to keep up with the latest fashions in footwear. Subsequently, the impoverished family were forced to move frequently (occupying nine different homes in ten years). Stalin's father was also an alcoholic who beat both his wife and son. Stalin's mother eventually took her child to stay with a family friend, Father Christopher Charkviani. Her ambition was that her son would be educated, something which no-one in the family had achieved thus far.

Father Charkviani helped to secure him a place at the local Church school and once there Stalin excelled academically. He progressed to a seminary college in Tiflis where he continued to excel. It was here that he began to lose his interest in theology and academia in favour of politics and economics. He was frequently confined for his rebellious behaviour which included claims to atheism and refusing to show deference to the monks. He joined a forbidden book club at school and it was through this club that he was exposed to Marxism. He read Marx's masterwork 'Das Capital' and became devoted to Marxism, eventually leaving the seminary in April 1899.

He took a job working as a meteorologist in Tiflis but was most committed to political activism. He began teaching socialist theory and by this means built up a following. Stalin successfully organised two strikes while working with underground groups in 1900 and 1901, becoming known to the government as a result. After escaping exile to Siberia he returned to Georgia to discover that the Marxist political party which he had been a member of (Russian Social Democratic Labour Party) had split into two factions. One of these was the Bolsheviks, a group to which Vladimir Lenin was associated. Stalin chose to ally himself with the Bolsheviks and this was the beginning of his association with Lenin. He became a full-time political agitator for the Bolshevik party, quickly rising through the ranks behind Lenin. When Lenin died in 1924, Stalin was in a senior position within the Central Committee of the Communist Party and was able to take control of the Party. He would become a brutal dictator.

Stalin began a policy of collectivisation in order to complete Russia's transition into a full communist state. All farms were collectivised and subject to government control. The government set about changing the direction of the Russian, largely agrarian, economy to transform it into an industrial one. This would lead to a famine in 1932 and 1933 in which millions would die. Millions more farmers, who resisted the seizure of their lands, would be arrested and murdered for their resistance. These farmers would have remembered the days of labouring as serfs on lands owned by the Czar, had briefly been given the rights to their own property but now saw them taken away again.

Between 1934 and 1939 any who voiced an opposition to Stalin was arrested, imprisoned and executed. Millions were killed to destroy any opposition to the Stalinist regime. He instituted a powerful secret police to root out opponents to his leadership and created intelligence agencies that would operate both within and without the Soviet Union. The full collectivisation of the Soviet Union could not be achieved and maintained without total government control of every aspect of society and Stalin believed that it could not survive without the complete eradication of dissent. He achieved this with shocking brutality and is believed to responsible for the deaths of as many as twenty million of his own people.

5.6 - Aftermath

The Russian revolution began as an uprising by a downtrodden populace against a wealthy and decadent elite presiding over an antiquated, medieval feudal system. Had the revolution ceased with the Kerensky government then today it might earn comparisons with the 'Glorious Revolution' of England in 1688. The Kerensky government sought to create a system of constitutional monarchy in which the Czars power was limited and an elected body (the 'duma') represented the people. By this means, social reform could have been achieved gradually as it had been by the English, with basic freedoms and rights of the people secured within a written bill of rights. Such a revolution had proved successful in England and, to a lesser degree, in Turkey as it transitioned from the former Ottoman Empire.

However, the Russian revolution had been motivated in part by a radical movement within the working classes inspired by the work of Marx. The Bolsheviks within the new government were driven by the new socialist philosophy that Marx had formulated and they were not satisfied by the moderate Kerensky government. The Bolsheviks were radicals, prepared to embrace extreme violence to achieve their ends, including the perpetration of organised crime in order to fund their cause. In Georgia, a young Josef Stalin had organised 'Battle Squads' from his Bolshevik followers for the purposes of raising funds through armed robbery and protection racketeering. They also attacked barracks and police stations to obtain weapons and to ensure the local authorities had no power to oppose them. The Bolsheviks wanted to go much further than the provisional revolutionary government. This would lead to an outburst of violence in which the Kerensky government would be swept aside.

Led first by Lenin the Bolsheviks seized power and tore down the remains of the old regime. Lenin desired a socialist state but was not radical enough to believe he could implement a fully collectivist state in one move.

He was prepared to accept compromise in his nationalisation and centralisation of the economy, allowing for the ownership of private property on a small scale. But, as his successor would prove to be, Lenin was fully prepared to accept bloodshed and death on a wide scale to achieve his ends. The Bolshevik revolutionaries believed that end justified means.

As a result, to separate Church and State and ensure the former Russian Orthodox Church could pose no Counter-Revolutionary threat, members of the church were arrested and imprisoned in concentration camps. Trotsky was given a free hand to mould his peasant army into a formidable fighting force and pursue the 'White' forces of the counter-revolution. While Lenin did ensure that Russia withdrew from the carnage of the First World War, his successor would prove a butcher on an unprecedented scale.

Josef Stalin would permit no compromise or threats to his power. Stalin represents the inevitable conclusion of the communist revolution. To institute a communist state requires total government control of the state. Stalin achieved this at the expense of millions of deaths from famine, as a result of the forcible conversion of the Russian economy from agriculture to industry. Millions more were persecuted and murdered to consolidate his power base, including former revolutionary leaders such as Trotsky. Stalin was a man who had spent his life immersed in violent actions in order to bring about the political and economic order which he believed was right. This was achieved at a high cost in human life

Ultimately, a revolution inspired by a radical philosophy would prove to be one of the bloodiest in human history. From Kerensky to Lenin to Stalin was a step by step progression following the tenets of Marx to their ultimate conclusion, a Soviet state that would dominate world politics for the next fifty years. That Soviet state would dominate its people, repressing freedom of speech and the press as a dangerous innovation that was at odds with the maintenance of the Communist party. Under the Communist system, people could not be allowed to exercise choice, or they may choose to leave, to protest or to undermine the system. For the greater good of the state, this could not be allowed to happen. The death toll over fifty years of state-sponsored oppression makes the Russian revolution one of the bloodiest of all time.

During World War II, the Soviet Union would be a key ally in its refusal to surrender to the might of the German war machine. It would bring Germany to its knees but one of the reasons Stalin was able to achieve this was an apparent disregard for the value of the individual lives of his citizens. The Red Army was able to draw on millions upon millions of reinforcements and throw them into impossible odds, sure in the knowledge that the state must survive. Stalin represents the perfect Soviet. The lives of tens of millions of Soviet citizens were clearly less important to him than victory and the spread of Communism. Only the threat of the atomic bomb could ultimately stop him from pursuing the war against the United States after their alliance came to an end. He is the logical end product of the Marxist revolution, as interpreted by Lenin and others. The Communist party was elevated to supremacy above all else in the Soviet Union with increasing repression utilised to disguise the fact that the communist system didn't work as effectively as the capitalist system. A liberal, free democracy in America was far more productive than the totalitarian regime produced by the Russian Revolution and this could not be allowed to be discovered.

The final cost of the Russian Revolution would be a deep-seated suspicion between Russia and the West, born of the decades of Cold War and ideological opposition. That veiled hostility may yet cost more lives going forward.

CHAPTER 6

THE IRANIAN REVOLUTION

Introduction

The Iranian Revolution was the culmination of a series of events which led to the overthrow of the Pahlavi dynasty as the ruling family of the country. Rule by the 'Shah' was ended after two thousand five hundred years of monarchical rule. Iran became an Islamic republic ruled by the 'Ayatollah'.

6.1 - The Ulama

Until 1921 Iran was known by its ancient name, Persia. The country became Muslim in 651 after conquest by the Arab Caliphs in the seventh century. It would be a Sunni nation until the ascension of the Safavid dynasty in 1501, at which point the Shi'a faith became dominant and would remain the dominant religion to this day. Under the Shi'a rule, other Islamic faiths were forcibly converted or killed. This period saw the rise to power of the 'ulama'. These were Shi'a clerics who formed a religious elite within Persian society.

The 'ulama' became more than just the leaders of the church and custodians of Islam. They occupied high social, economic and political positions. It was the 'ulama' who formed the inner circle of advisors to the Persian 'Shah' (King) as well as occupying the highest offices of state. Successive shahs would use the 'ulama' to legitimise their rule. By ensuring 'ulama' support for their policies they would ensure the support of the people, who were guided by the clerics. An example of 'ulama' power was a deal struck by the Shah Nasir-al Din to grant a monopoly on the production and export of tobacco to the British in 1891. This would have been detrimental to the interests of the almost 200,000 Persian tobacco farmers and workers and was opposed by widespread protests. These protests were organised and led by the 'ulama' and proved successful. The Shah was forced to cancel the concession in face of the widespread popular protest.

It was in this period, the late nineteenth century that Persian saw their country being effectively sold off piecemeal by a Shah desperate for foreign money. In particular, the British and the Russians were dividing the country between them. This caused unrest and protests in which the 'ulama' played a central role and culminating in 1906 when the first Parliament of Persia was formed. However, this first elected body proved relatively ineffective in representing the people or curbing the foreign powers interference in Persia.

6.2 - Reza Khan

The power of the 'ulama' was threatened with the downfall of the Qajar dynasty in 1921. A coup was orchestrated by Reza Khan which ousted the ruling Qajar dynasty from the throne. Reza Khan was named Prime Minister in 1923 and then crowned Shah in 1925 to become Reza Pahlavi Shah. It was Reza who changed the name of the country from Persia to Iran. He wanted to modernise Iran, to implement a strong, centralised government that would be capable of delivering a comprehensive program of state education and infrastructure investment. He also desired Iran to be a secular country where church and state were effectively separated. In this, he was influenced by the work of Kemal Attaturk in forging the nation of Turkey, as a secular nation.

Reza wanted to model Iran on the Western nations, creating a modern, Western-style economy with manufacturing industries, banks, communication networks and a retail sector. He presided over the construction of a trans-Iranian railroad and expansion of the oil industry. The University of Iran was founded under Reza Khan and the creation of a national education system and a judiciary which was modelled on the French system.

Reza began filling government posts with secular appointments, recognising that the 'ulama' monopoly on government jobs could not continue. To create a strong infrastructure he needed able men, not clerics who possessed no qualifications for the posts they held other than their position within the Islamic faith. Reza also sought to reform the role of women in Iranian society. He wanted women to play a bigger role, one that would not just be limited to the home.

This was met with heavy resistance from the 'ulama' because of the departure it signalled from Islamic tradition and Shari'a law. Reza Shah sought to further modernise Iran and undermine the religious elite by banning the wearing of traditional Muslim clothes, passing a law in December 1828 to require Western clothes to be worn. Female teachers were banned from covering their heads and the sexes were encouraged to mix. In 1934 it was made possible to levy heavy fines against cinemas, restaurants and cafes who refused to allow the mixing of men and women on their premises. These policies led to a mass protest of clerics at the Mashed (a populous Iranian city) shrine. The protest lasted for four days before Iranian Azerbaijani troops attacked the mosque killing dozens and injuring hundreds more. This marked a watershed moment for the relationship between the 'ulama' and the Shah.

Ultimately, Reza was undone by foreign interests, especially the British. At the outbreak of the Second World War, Reza was inclined to support the Axis powers. Despite the creation of a Parliament structure in the 1906 Constitutional Revolution, Iran under the Pahlavi dynasty was essentially a military dictatorship. The Parliament was largely symbolic, with real power residing in the Shah as it had always done. This meant that Reza Shah found himself sympathetic to the Nazis, and this, in turn, led to his removal from the throne by the British.

6.3 - Mossadegh

Reza Shah was succeeded by his son Mohammed on September 16th, 1941. In order to avoid his father's fate, Mohammad Reza Shah was keen to ally himself with the Allied powers during the war. Iran became a shipping conduit for British and American forces to deliver supplies to the Soviet Union. While this strengthened his ties with the Western allies it also damaged his standing with his own people. He was regarded as a puppet of the West and the legitimacy of his rule was called into question. Mohammad Reza Shah found he had plenty of opponents to his rule, created during his father's reign.

On April 28th, 1941 the Iranian parliament elected Mohammed Mossadegh as it's Prime Minister. He had served as a politician in the Iranian Parliament for more than twenty years in various capacities. He had voted against the proposal of Prime Minister Reza Khan to dissolve the Qajar dynasty and make himself ruler of the country, claiming that this was against the constitution agreed in 1906. When Reza Shah took power he retired from politics and remained in retirement until Reza Shah's removal from power and the succession of his son.

Mossadegh was part of a movement known as the National Front, a party capable of mobilising strikes and protests from among socialists, Islamists and working people of Iran. He wanted to free Iran from foreign control, specifically the British and Americans. Though Iran was a sovereign nation, its oil reserves and strategic location meant that it had always been of interest to Western powers. Successive Shahs had accepted foreign money paid to them personally in exchange for concessions which amounted to selling off Iran's natural resources. Iran was treated almost as a colonial possession by the British, a source of commercial exploitation.

Mossadegh's first objective was the nationalisation of the Anglo-Iranian Oil Company (AIOC). This concession had been arranged with the British by Reza Shah in 1933 and was highly profitable for them but not for Iran. It was nationalised on the 1st May with all of its assets seized by Iran. Britain responded with a naval and economic blockade to prevent Iran from selling any of the oil it had seized. AIOC workers were ordered from their jobs and the Iranian administration lacked the resources to continue operating the refineries and wells.

Iranian oil production fell to almost zero amid plans to introduce sweeping social reforms which would have greatly benefited ordinary working Iranians at the expense of property owners. Despite the economic crisis caused by the nationalisation of AIOC Mossadegh remained popular, especially among the urban classes. He called elections on the 28th April 1851 to consolidate his power base, only to call off the elections before all of the required deputies to Parliament had been selected. The National Front dominated those that had been chosen. Mossadegh cited foreign involvement in the electoral process designed to bring down his government as his reason for ceasing the elections when he did. There is some evidence to suggest that the American CIA was active in generating opposition against Mossadegh among the provincial classes and the 'ulama' on behalf of the British.

The result was that Mossadegh remained in power and on the 16th July 1952, while waiting for the Shah to ratify his cabinet choices, he insisted that it was within the power of the Prime Minister to choose a Minister for War and Chief of Staff for the military. This had previously been within the purview of the Shah and Mohammad Reza Shah refused on the grounds that it would give the Prime Minister an unshakeable power base with control over the military. Mossadegh resigned in protest, making his decision very public. The National Front mobilised their supporters and a coalition of nationalists, socialists and Islamists took to the streets of Tehran and other cities.

There were around two hundred and fifty deaths in urban areas during the period of unrest, as the military was called on to restore order. Finally, Mossadegh was reinstated and order restored. Over the next two years, he set about passing a series of laws that would limit the power of the monarchy and social reforms of the almost feudal, agricultural society of rural Iran. Unsettled by the violence and unrest, the Shah reinstated Mossadegh to his position as Prime Minister.

Mossadegh proceeded to campaign for, and got, emergency powers that allowed him to pass any laws he chose. He used these powers to restrict the powers of the Shah, forbid him from contact with foreign diplomats and restricted his personal budget. Going further, he established village councils and increased the share of production to which land workers were entitled from the land they worked. This social reform was designed to increase his support amongst the rural working classes.

Mossadegh did this with a coalition of support in the Parliament which included the 'Tudeh' party, which was the Iranian communist party. His alliance with the Tudeh Party combined with his nationalisation and social reform programme would be his eventual undoing. It alarmed the Americans in particular, now on the lookout for countries that might align themselves with the Soviet Union. America would have been very conscious that Reza Shah had begun his military career with Red Army training and that links may still exist between the Iranian military and the Soviets.

With the election of President Eisenhower in the United States, the view of potential Communist links in the Iranian government was viewed more seriously than under previous administrations. The British had been lobbying for American support removing Mossadegh for power and under Eisenhower, they got the help they were looking for. The CIA orchestrated mass demonstrations in the streets of Tehran and lined up a political successor to Mossadegh in General Fazlollah Zahedi. They also bribed the Shah's family in order to pressure him into issuing a decree removing Mossadegh from power.

The Shah agreed in August 1953 and the coup was launched which resulted in the arrest of Mossadegh. Another factor in his overthrow was the dissolution of the coalition he had built within Parliament. Instrumental to this was Ayatollah Abol-Gasem Kashani, a leading cleric who had supported the nationalisation of APOC but become concerned over the socialist leanings of Mossadegh's subsequent legislation and his alliance with the Tudeh party. Kashani was rightly wary of any potential communist takeover, given the known views of communism towards religion and the separation of church and state. Without the support of the 'ulama' Mossadegh lost the support of the people and the Americans were able to remove him from power.

The division between the secular government and the 'ulama', the interference of foreign powers in Iranian politics and the exploitation of Iran by foreign commercial interests would all be factors in the revolution that would take place just over twenty years later. The period of upheaval that began with the Constitutional Revolution and the creation of a Parliamentary body; the coup that put the Pahlavi dynasty on the throne; the undermining of a nationalist Prime Minister by foreign powers in order that they may continue to commercially exploit the country were all factors in the revolution of 1979 and the wide-ranging consequences that would have and continues to have on world politics.

6.4 - Mohammad Reza Shah Pahlavi

The Shah had fled Iran after issuing his decree removing Mossadegh from power. He feared the civil unrest and death threats that had been the result of the last time he had attempted to remove Mossadegh from power. His temporary exile had been provided courtesy of the United States and he owed his return to power to America as well. This would not have been lost on his opponents, and unlikely that it would have been unknown to the people too.

Understandably given that he owed his throne to the US and his succession to his father to the British, Mohammed Reza was keen to align his country with the West. In the 1950's this meant alignment with the United States. To regain control of his country, the Parliament was stripped of powers and the British oil companies allowed to go back to their exploitation. Mohammad Reza followed the iron hand of his father and ruled as an autocrat. He was determined to build up a power base that could not be shaken as his father's had been.

He used US military advisors and weapons to build an accomplished, well-armed, well-resourced military force. He also formed a secret police, known as the SAVAK, to seek out and crush dissident voices brutally. Initially dismissed by British and American intelligence agencies as weak and a coward, Mohammad Reza Shah proved an adept politician. He manipulated the United States into granting more support to his leadership by threatening a non-aggression pact with the Soviet Union. He was also able to neutralise his opponent General Fazlollah Zahedi, mindful of the route which his own father had taken to the throne (from military to Prime Minister to Shah).

Adopting the policies of his opponents, such as the National Front, he publicly declared his desire for social reform, condemning the third world poverty which prevailed in rural Iran. By this means he took away his opponents platform, while he then commuted death sentences for dissidents taken by his secret police, and so appeared just and magnanimous. This was a pretence, by the 1970's the SAVAK had more than two thousand political prisoners in detention.

6.5 - White Revolution

In 1963 Mohammad Reza Shah launched his 'White Revolution'. This was an attempt to mollify the 'ulamas' that his father had so antagonised. This was a series of social reforms based on the five basic needs; health, food, clothing, housing and education. He emphasised that it was necessary to reform Iranian society in order for Iran to retain its place among the free and progressive nations of the world. He described his vision as one based on spiritual principles and religious beliefs, as well as individual freedoms. The reforms of the 'White Revolution' were applauded by the United States, with two presidents extending personal congratulations to the Shah (Kennedy and Johnson).

It is clear from the Shah's own autobiography that despite his care in phrasing the 'White Revolution' as taking place hand in hand with the spiritual and religious aspects of Iranian society, he did not expect to gain the support of the 'ulama'. The Shah described how he believed they would attempt to sabotage his reforms, and that it was in their interests to ensure Iran remained an impoverished, rural country over which they held a great deal of power. In his 'White Revolution,' Mohammad Reza Shah could use the right words to fit in with the progressive leaders of the free world. But his actions showed his true nature, an autocrat like his father. He swept away the Iranian Parliament in order to ensure no obstacles to his plans for freedom and liberty. He suspended future elections and then set about his reforms personally.

This Shah, like his father, had an obsession with taking personal control of the state. In an effort to take away the moral authority, social and political power of the 'ulama' he created the 'Sipah-i Din', or 'Religious Corps'. They had their own mosques and Imams and were responsible for the promotion of the 'Din-i Dawlat', the Government Religion. The 'Religious Corps' would serve to show that the Shah placed as much importance on the spiritual as he did on the material reforms taking place as part of the 'White Revolution'. The Shah had brought about female suffrage, improved infrastructure and technology and improved literacy. He was now about to reform the Iranian religion.

The implementation of the 'Religious Corps' infuriated the 'ulama' and caused them to become leaders of the opposition to the Shah. This opposition would soon turn to revolution.

6.6 - Khomeini

Ruhollah Khomeini would become the face of the Iranian Revolution and in the western media the face of evil. He was born on September 24th, 1902. He began his Islamic education at a young age, attending a seminary and in 1923, at the age of twenty-one, continuing his education in the city of Qom. As the Pahlavi dynasty began to break apart the old Iranian regime, stripping the 'ulama' of their power, he became a teacher. He was elevated from obscurity to a position of prominence in March 1961 following the death of Ayatollah Boroujedi, the most prominent cleric in Qom. Khomeini began publishing his work on Islamic doctrine and law which led to him being seen as a respected scholar and religious leader. He became accepted as a 'Marja-e Taqlid', a position of high seniority within the Shi-ite clerics.

This was significant for a Shi'ite because a 'Marja' could not be elected or appointed but was chosen by each individual from among the clergy. Whoever was judged to be the most knowledgeable and pious would be chosen 'Marja'. Khomeini was regarded as 'Marja' by a majority of Iranians, meaning that a significant majority of Iranians chose to follow him. In 1962, now occupying a very public position, Khomeini began to speak out against the regime of Mohammad Reza Shah. Previously he had felt in no position to speak the outrage he had felt against the regime because he lacked the stature within the clergy to take such a stand.

In 1962, he organised a protest against the proposed law that elected officials would not be required to be sworn in on the Qur'an. In June 1963 he made a speech critical of the 'White Revolution' and was arrested. This led to popular unrest and a protest calling for his release. He was released from prison in April 1964. By November, he had been arrested for a second time, again for making speeches critical of the Shah. He was immediately transported to Tehran and exiled to Turkey, later to move to Iraq where he would spend the next thirteen years as an exile. The Shah's government had believed that arresting and incarcerating Khomeini in Iran would make him the centre of popular protest but that exile would lead to him being forgotten.

This did not happen. Khomeini continued making speeches and writing. His works were published across Iraq and smuggled into Iran. He gave lectures in Iraq which received a wide, popular attendance. In Iran, protests against the regime continued, still using Khomeini as their figurehead. It was during this period of exile that Khomeini developed a theory of the perfect Islamic state. He called it 'Velayat-e Faqih' or 'Government of the Islamic Jurists'. It was a state based on Islamic principles and led by a member of the clergy with supreme knowledge of Islamic law. Mohammad Reza Shah realised that Khomeini was still a threat and arranged with Iraq for his deportation.

Khomeini was forced to leave Iraq in September 1978 and, realising that the Shah would pursue him in any Middle Eastern state, decided to move to France. He became a world famous figure thanks to the liberal media and free press enjoyed in the West. Journalists were free to visit him and report his words. Khomeini now had a world stage for his protests against the Shah, though he did not make public exactly what he envisioned would replace the monarchy. Khomeini would be a figurehead for many secular opposition groups within Iran because he shared their desire for the overthrow of the Shah and a new, just government in his place. These secular groups did not know that Khomeini wanted to create an Islamic republic in place of the monarchy, with supreme power resting in the clerics and himself, a system that would prove just as repressive and brutal as the Shah.

6.7 - Mourning Marches

At the same time, Mohammad Reza Shah was being forced by his Western allies to reform the more unpalatable aspects of his regime. He had modelled his new Iran on the Western nations but ruled as an autocrat, using the tools of a totalitarian. To show that he could take his place among liberal, Western leaders he announced that free and fair elections would be held in 1978, and invited human rights groups to inspect Iranian prisons to see how the inmates were treated. Those who opposed the Shah took advantage of the weakening of the regime, which coincided with Khomeini's well-publicized views and protests. Opposition groups began to emerge and make their voices heard publicly. One of these was a left-leaning, secular group, the Iranian Writers Association. They staged a sit-in at the Goethe Institute in Tehran. The protest was attacked by security forces leading to several deaths.

In October 1977, shortly after the Iran Writers Association's protest, the son of Khomeini, Mostafa Khomeini, died of a heart attack. There were rumours that this was an assassination orchestrated by SAVAK. The death of Mostafa produced demonstrations in Tehran by clerics and Khomeini supporters. The police dispersed protesters amid mounting arrests but this just added fuel to the fire. Political rallies sprang up all over Iran, driven by the rumours surrounding Mostafa Khomeini's death. The protests continued into 1978. In January, the Shah arranged for a propaganda article to be published in the Iranian newspaper 'Ittila'at' which accused Khomeini of being a British agent and a homosexual, as well as of being Indian by birth, not Iranian. The article produced a backlash among radical students, clerics and other Khomeini supporters who took to the streets of Qom in their thousands. More deaths were the result as security forces dispersed them. Seventy protesters were killed.

Protesters adopted a forty day period of mourning for the massacre was instituted by the protestors. Mourning marches took place across sixteen Iranian cities on February 19th, 1978. In Tehran, the march turned bloody as protesters clashed with security forces. These clashes were becoming a regular occurrence, and accounts of them were distributed across Iran to further inflame new protests. In June 1978 the decision was taken to halt the mourning marches for fear of the mounting death toll. Despite the cessation of the protests, the damage to the regime had been done already.

6.8 - Overthrow of the Shah

Khomeini was viewed as the leader of the opposition in Iran and, following the slanderous article published by 'Ittila'at', these protests were lead by the Islamic clerics. Prior to this, it had been socialists and intellectuals who had led the protests and had petitioned the Shah. However, the clumsy attempt to defame Khomeini led to the opposition being taken by the 'ulama' and taking on an Islamist timbre. In August 1978 a fire broke out at a cinema in the city of Abadan in southwestern Iran. 377 people were killed in the blaze which the government blamed on the opposition and the opposition blamed on SAVAK. This, in turn, led to further widespread protests to which the Shah responded either with brutal repression or half-hearted conciliation.

He restored the Islamic calendar, which he had previously tried to abolish, lifted the restrictions of the press and once again promised free elections. But at the same time, clerics continued to be persecuted when they spoke out against the regime and SAVAK continued with arrests and beatings of activists and protesters. In September 1978, the Shah appointed General Gholam-Ali Oveissi as military governor of Tehran. His first act was to declare martial law, but this was ignored by protestors who gathered in Jaleh square on September 8th. Security forces were sent in and over an estimated three thousand people were killed as the attempt to clear the square became a running battle. Police fired into the crowd, many of whom sat on the ground and bared their chests. Helicopters were used to attack slums in the south of Tehran. It came to be remembered as 'Black Friday'.

Black Friday served to radicalise all within the various opposition groups. There was now no turning back. In the second half of 1978, a series of strikes began which would blend into a general strike that would paralyze the Iranian economy. This began in October 1978 and covered crucial oil workers as well as workers in other industries. As more and more joined the strike so there was a domino effect elsewhere. Because of customs strikes, imported ink couldn't be delivered to the Iranian treasury who could produce no new currency. As a result, this led to a shortage of actual currency available which in turn led to companies and even industries shutting down as they could not pay either workers or suppliers.

Khomeini recognised the importance of embracing the strikes. They were a means of destabilising the regime which the Shah could not counter. His tactic of repression and concession did not satisfy the striking workers and repression could not force them to work anyway. At the end of November 1978, Khomeini publicly endorsed the general strike and urged the strikers to continue until the Shah abdicated. In the Muslim month of 'Muharram' (around December) the demonstrations in the streets of Iranian cities reached a new peak. Between the 10th and 11th of December one million people marched peacefully through the streets of Tehran. They carried pictures of Khomeini. Across the country as a whole, an estimated six million took to the streets to peacefully demand the abdication of the Shah.

The Shah approached a moderate member of the opposition, Shapour Bakhtiar, to form a new liberal government and appease the people. Bakhtiar agreed on the condition that the Shah left the country. Mohammad Reza Shah Pahlavi abdicated his throne and left Iran on the 16th January 1979. Bakhtiar formed a new government and began implementing liberal policies such as the freedom of the press, the liberation of political prisoners and the dismantling of the SAVAK. Khomeini wasn't satisfied, however, seeing Bakhtiar as another Shah appointed minister who would not allow the Ayatollah to create his Islamic state. He refused to endorse Bakhtiar's government and announced his return to Tehran.

The new government closed the airport at Tehran to prevent this and Khomeini supporters clashed with the army, resulting in deaths. This was the perfect opportunity for Khomeini to publicly condemn the Prime Minister as being a carbon copy of the Shah, willing to kill to enforce his will on the people. On February 1st, 1979, Khomeini returned to Iran and named his own government which was in direct competition to that of Bakhtiar. The army declared its neutrality in the contest on February 11th, a message to the incumbent government that they would not have military help against Khomeini's followers. Bakhtiar fled into hiding and Khomeini was free to take power and begin to build his Islamic republic.

6.9 - Aftermath

In the immediate aftermath of the overthrow of the Shah and his chosen replacement, there was a great deal of political chaos. However, Khomeini took just a matter of months to impose order and create a system whereby he became Supreme Leader, backed by bodies of 'ulama'. He appointed a Prime Minister and Cabinet, but then created a Revolutionary Council which held effective power over the Prime Minister. In May 1979 the Revolutionary Guard was formed, replacing the SAVAK but performing the same function. Tribunals were set up across Iran to try members of the pre-revolutionary government. A referendum was held on April 1st, 1979 to determine which type of government the people of Iran wanted. There was only one option on the ballot, Islamic Republic. Unsurprisingly, 98% of Iranians voted for it despite having no information on what an Islamic republic actually was.

When the Shah was admitted to the United States for cancer treatment there was widespread protest in Iran, fearing this was a pretext for an attempt to return the Shah to power. This led to the hostage crisis at the Iranian embassy in Tehran on November 4th, 1979. On November 6th the Prime Minister appointed by Khomeini resigned and the old constitution was swept away. Under the new constitution, Iran would have a figurehead President while supreme power rested in the Ayatollah. The Iranian Islamic Republic would be one where the Muslim clergy would be restored to their position as the ruling elite of Iranian society. As an Islamic regime and the only Islamic republic in the world (one whose government was based on the principles of Islam rather than any liberal or democratic philosophies) Khomeini saw it as his duty to spread his message across the world.

He believed there was only one kind of nation and governmental system that was proper and that was the Islamic Republic. He urged the Shi'a population of Iraq to rise against their Sunni government (the regime of Saddam Hussein). Perhaps feeling threatened by this or merely taking advantage of the initial disorder following the revolution, but Hussein invaded Iran, leading to an eight-year war. By the end of the Iran-Iraq war in 1988, 300,000 Iranians had died and around 800,000 Iraqis. It is certain that this war could not have taken place under the Shah, not least because the Western powers who sponsored his regime would not allow such a destabilising conflict to begin. The Iran-Iraq war was a direct consequence of the revolution and the incredible death toll of that conflict can be added to that of the revolution itself, just as the casualties of the Napoleonic Wars can be laid at the door of the French Revolution which spawned his regime.

But the Iranian Revolution did more than give birth to a terrible regional war. It legitimised an idea which has come to have dire consequences to the western world. It made concrete the idea of the Islamic republic, the Caliphate where Islamic law is supreme. This is the philosophy that has been claimed by such groups as Al-Qaeda and, of course, the eponymously named Islamic State. From the philosophy conceived by a junior Iranian cleric in the 1950's has come some of the most brutal terrorist atrocities of our modern era. Iran was freed from the shackles of an autocrat who ruled on behalf of exploitative international corporations and Western superpowers, to be placed in new chains by it's supposed, liberator. The Iranian revolution was distinct in history as one which restored the old regime at the expense of the new. It spawned a medieval philosophy of government which some still try to spread by force and which has caused death and suffering across the world to this day.

CHAPTER 7

THE HAITIAN REVOLUTION

Introduction

The Haitian Revolution was an uprising by self-freed slaves in the French Caribbean colony of Saint Domingue. It occurred between 1791 and 1804 and involved an armed insurrection by black and mulatto slaves against the colonial rule of the French. The Haitian Revolution occupies a unique space among a history of eighteenth and nineteenth-century revolutions, and in particular slave revolutions. It is the only revolt by self-freed slaves which resulted in the birth of a free nation, governed by non-whites. It occurred after the American War of Independence in 1776 and the French Revolution of 1789.

This places the Haitian revolution amid a period of global unrest in which the supremacy of the Western European powers, and their ruling elites, was being challenged. American colonists had stood up to the might of the British army and navy to win their independence, while French peasants had succeeded in overthrowing the absolute monarchy of Louis XVI, tearing down the entire apparatus of church and state in the process. When viewed through this lens it is easy to see how the uprising of black slaves in a profitable colony, belonging to a European imperial power,

105

would be a cause for great concern for the powers that be. It was symbolic of the decline of the old orders that had governed European society, and by extension European colonies, for centuries. It was also a warning to those nations that still relied on a black slave economy, notably the United States.

The success of the revolution in overthrowing the French rule and creating a new, independent country (Haiti) governed by former slaves, and black slaves at that, would cause fear and consternation throughout the United States and Europe. The violence which the revolutionaries practised in order to secure their freedom was incidental, though would play its part in scaremongering to come. If the slaves of Saint Domingue could overthrow those who held them in bondage then what might the far more numerous slaves in the southern United States be capable of?

7.1 - Saint Domingue

The island that would come to be known as Saint Domingue began as a Spanish settlement discovered by Christopher Columbus in 1492. It was named 'Hispaniola' but it was largely ignored by Spain in favour of its mainland American conquests. With little deterrence from the Spanish, pirates established bases on nearby Tortuga and the western half of Hispaniola. In 1606, the Spanish King ordered that all Spanish subjects should concentrate on the settlement of Saint Domingo in order to avoid interaction with pirate elements in the west. This allowed for the French to establish themselves there, first as an illegitimate pirate presence, then as a formal Crown colony. This occurred in 1665 and was finally acknowledged as such by the Spanish in 1697. It was discovered that tobacco could be grown there, and the emergence of a tobacco economy and the 'safe' money that could be made from the tobacco trade led to Saint Domingue moving from a home to freebooters and pirates, to one of plantation owners and farmers. The French population, in particular, began to increase as more and more white Europeans arrived to make their fortune. These fortunes increased significantly when tobacco was supplanted by an even more in demand and lucrative cash crop, sugar. Over the next century, the French economy became increasingly dependent on the agriculture of its overseas colonies, because of the highly valued nature of the produce.

Black slaves from West Africa were imported to fuel the labour intensive plantation economy and the economic value of the island rapidly increased. As well as its main cash crops of coffee and, particularly, sugar there was a thriving market for cocoa, coconuts and snuff; all of which could be produced on the island. Saint Domingue earned the nickname 'Pearl of the Antilles' thanks to the immense wealth its agriculture began to produce for the French crown. It was a major port in the flow of trade to and from France and the Americas and a significant contributor to the French national budget.

The most valuable crops were labour intensive and so were grown on huge plantations in order to maximise profits. Slaves provided the most cost-effective workforce. In the case of sugar cane plantations, in particular, the work was murderous. Slaves from West Africa were in plentiful supply and it was more economical for slave owners to work their slaves to death and replace them rather than conserve their existing workforce. This produced a harsh environment in Saint Domingue, one which would produce a vengeful backlash and a revolt that would match the cruelty of the slave owners in its brutality.

People of colour outnumbered whites on the island but that majority was not composed entirely of slaves. There was a population of freed blacks on Saint Domingue as well as mixed-race people who were the children of white fathers and black mothers. These children were often freed from slavery by their fathers and provided with education. They would eventually form a new class in Saint Domingue society, in between the white elite and the black slaves. Some slaves sought to escape the harsh life on the plantations and found a haven in the mountainous central regions. These runaway slaves would often end up interbreeding with the indigenous population and formed independent settlements. They became knowns as 'maroons' and would form a significant population in that area.

The white, French elite of Saint Domingue were excessively wealthy, so valuable were the products the island produced to the American and European markets. By the 1780's forty percent of all the sugar and sixty percent of all coffee consumed in Europe had its origins on the island of Saint Domingue. The French nation itself also benefited greatly from the wealth of its colony. But on the island itself the divisions between the rich, white elite, black slaves or maroons was marked. The class divisions and the cruel life which blacks were forced to lead would be the catalysts of revolution, just as they would be for the native French in their own revolution.

7.2 - Francois Mackandal

In 1751 a slave named Francois Mackandal escaped from his master and fled to the centre of the island. He became a maroon. He had been born in Africa where he was a religious man and a leader. He became so again in Saint Domingue. Under Mackandal's leadership, several maroon communities were united and they began a campaign to liberate the rest of the island's slaves. For seven years, the plantations were raided, whites killed and slaves freed. Mackandal talked of revolution and a slave insurrection, something which terrified the white minority. Before he was captured and executed in 1758, he and his followers killed six thousand people. He was burned at the stake to set a brutal example.

7.3 - Race and Class

The class system in Saint Domingue, with its mix of white, black and mixed race, was tied up with race. Whites ruled but bestowed property and money on mixed-race children. It was these mixed race people that formed the majority of a class of coloured free men known as the 'gens de couleur'. In fact, despite the dominance of the whites on Saint Domingue, the island did possess the largest free population of colour of any Caribbean colony. The prosperity of that child would depend on the degree of white blood they possessed. A complicated system arose to officially determine a person's racial status, and therefore their position in the social pecking order. The more black, the lower down. The system was made more complicated by corruption, with money changing hands to ensure documentation proving the purity of their 'white' heritage.

In the wake of Mackandal's insurrection, the white population of Saint Domingue were fearful of the black majority they depended on for their livelihoods. They were also becoming concerned about the systemic corruption that was allowing more and more mixed race people to rise to the elite, even though their ethnicity should have prevented them. It was a system created by the whites but was now serving to aid those ethnic groups they wanted to keep in their place. The threat of revolt was always present, thanks to the brigand maroons. They lived primarily off their lands but needed to raid the plantations from time to time. Sometimes they raids erupted into violence.

There was also a growing population of free blacks, some of whom were property owners and accruing respectable fortunes for themselves. They did not have the rights of the white plantations owners but nothing in law barred them from ownership of property. The island was a powder keg, with a coloured underclass forced to take arms to feed themselves and a disenfranchised, brutalised, tortured majority on whose hard work everybody else depended. Overall of this was an increasingly paranoid white population who felt that harsh penalties and a rule of iron were the only ways to keep the majority in power.

7.4 - The French Revolution

The French Revolution in 1789 was a catalyst for the later Haitian Revolution in 1791. Or rather, its ideas were a catalyst. In particular the 'Declaration of the Rights of Man. To the white planters of Saint Domingue, the Declaration meant that their rights to property were strengthened and guaranteed. They were born equal and so their wealth, land and slave workforce could not be taken from them by the arbitrary will of a monarch. They also believed that they had the freedom to trade with whom they wished, rather than being forced only to sell to France (as their position as a French colony existed solely to benefit the mother country).

Though hardly able to read reports of the French Revolution or reproductions of the Declaration the black population of Saint Domingue would have heard news of the uprising and the new ideas which had come into being with it. People talk, white planters would certainly have been discussing it and this talk would have reached the ears of freed blacks and slaves. In the south of Saint Domingue, mountains cut off the region from the rest of the island while the British colony of Jamaica was only a short distance across the sea. News would have reached the southern regions from the British and spread in that way too.

Either way, the black population will have heard of the revolutionary struggle in France and the concepts of liberty and, more importantly, equality. There was only one way a second class freed black citizen or a black slave could interpret those words. They were equal to the whites. The freed blacks were the first to take action. Leaders among these communities travelled to France to request assurances from the National Assembly that their equality and their property rights would be honoured alongside those of their white counterparts. In late 1790 a rebellion broke out on Saint Domingue led by the 'gens de couleur', literally 'gentlemen of colour' as the freed blacks were known.

It seems unlikely that this uprising was a colonial revolution against France, rather than a revolt against the whites on Saint Domingue. The rebels sought to fight for and hold their property, to present the government in France with a 'fait accompli'. They would secure their rights and request the government confirm their hard-won position. After all, that is what the revolutionaries in France had done. The revolt was crushed and it's leaders executed but it represented the beginning.

7.5 - The Slaves revolt

By 1791 the slaves of Saint Domingue had heard, through various means and against the wishes of their owners, of the French Revolution and the 'Declaration of the Rights of Man'. They would certainly have known of the maroon uprising of the 1750's which is likely to have achieved mythic proportions among an enslaved population and of the 'gens de couleur' revolt of 1790. If the freed blacks felt anxious to guarantee their rights and freedoms following the French Revolution then the slaves would have felt an even greater sense of urgency.

In February 1791, the French government allowed full citizenship to free people of colour. They must have reasoned that this would defuse any potential uprisings in the colonies by putting free blacks on a par with the whites. There would be no need for a free black population to rise against the white population, or worse still, against France itself, if they possessed truly equal rights and a stake as citizens in the republic.

The white population of Saint Domingue disagreed. They saw the extension of equal rights to the free blacks as being a threat to the institution of slavery. The white population was outnumbered by the population of free blacks and slaves. Equal rights would also threaten their elite status within the island's government. If freed blacks achieved a balance of power would they not seek to extend the freedoms they enjoyed to the slave population? This would threaten the way of life and the wealth of the white population.

From these fears came the decision to suppress the new law. The white elite refused to acknowledge its existence or put it into practice. This, in turn, angered the freed black population who saw their rights being denied and this led to violence between white and black. This violence would rapidly spiral into a full-fledged revolution. One of the flashpoints centred on a religious meeting in the north of the island, led by a slave named Dutty Boukman. He incited a slave rebellion on the 21st August 1791 and received a huge response.

Boukman's followers moved from plantation to plantation, their numbers growing each time as they liberated more slaves. In previous slave rebellions, in the Americas or Jamaica, for example, fear of retribution had prevented a mass rising. In Saint Domingue however, the slaves appeared to know that this was their opportunity. The uprising was rapid and by the 31st August, the rebels controlled the entire northern region of the island. As they liberated they also destroyed. They burnt the plantations which they had been enslaved too as well as the homes of the white landowners and the towns in which they lived. The slave rebels also enacted bloody retribution against the slave owners themselves for the way in which they had been treated. There was no quarter given and around four thousand whites were killed.

7.6 - Toussaint Louverture

Toussaint Louverture emerged as a leader of the freed slave rebels but at the beginning of the uprising, he was more of a neutral. He had been a slave himself, being granted his freedom in 1776. He was educated and so acted as a negotiator and go-between for the slave rebels and the white elite. Louverture helped whites escape the rebels wrath but also persuaded them to agree to the better treatment of slave prisoners.

By 1792, however, he found himself siding more and more with the slaves. By this point, they had gained control of two-thirds of the island. The French government had come to hear of the revolt and had despatched a large number of troops to suppress it. The cost of such a venture was justified because of the immense wealth the island was capable of producing for them. Revolution on Saint Domingue would mean economic ruin for France. By the time the French troops arrived the freed slaves had been organised by Louverture into a highly effective fighting force. In their favour, they were also fighting for their freedom and that of their families which gave them significantly greater motivation than the French troops sent far from home.

British and Spanish ships began supplying the rebels with arms and ammunition when both countries went to war with France in 1792. The Spanish had maintained a fortified enclave on the eastern side of the island since its discovery and now they crossed the island to join the rebels. The situation was untenable for the French. The rebels were well led, well-armed and supplied. They couldn't be beaten into submission, at least not while France's enemies continued to support the rebels.

In 1793 the French government abolished slavery both in France and in all her dominions. It was a decision hailed as a victory for the Enlightenment and the Revolution but it was also a move calculated to stop the revolution in Saint Domingue in its tracks. Having received the news that every man, woman and child in Saint Domingue were free, Louverture brought his army over to the French. After helping to defeat both the Spanish and British, and to secure the colony for France once again, Louverture persuaded his followers to return to the plantations. They would now be paid but would still be subject to the harsh conditions of such large scale, labour intensive agriculture. For Louverture however it was a demonstration that slave workforces were not required to make cash crop agriculture work. If Saint Domingue could continue to generate wealth for the French without slavery that it would demonstrate that the same could be done throughout the world.

Louverture did not surrender his position of leadership, having once again restored the island to French control. He worked assiduously to eliminate rivals to his leadership and consolidate his position. Towards the end of 1800, he led his followers to an invasion of the Spanish enclave of Santo Domingo without the permission of the French government. When Napoleon seized power in France and declared that he would change the laws, Louverture and the former slave rebels must have feared the reintroduction of slavery.

Louverture acted first by issuing a constitution for the island (including the former Spanish enclave) in 1801. From this constitution he was named Governor-General for life and that the island would be subject to home rule, though not at this point independent from France. If this constitution was intended to reassure the Emperor of Saint Domingue's loyalty it failed. Napoleon was not happy with the constitution when it was presented to him and despatched twenty thousand troops under General LeClerc to overthrow Louverture.

At the same time, the new constitution had not received universal acclaim at home. Louverture was forced to put down a rebellion of labourers in 1801 with significant loss of life. The black population of the island was no longer wholly united behind their charismatic leader. When the French troops arrived, fighting broke out among coastal towns and cities. Casualties were heavy, especially among civilians, so much so that both sides agreed to begin negotiations. By May 1802 a truce was agreed. Louverture agreed to surrender his troops in exchange for his freedom. He went into retirement on his plantation. However, by the end of the month, he had been arrested and imprisoned. Napoleon was not prepared to tolerate an anti-slavery, liberationist alive and in a position to make further trouble for the Empire.

Louverture died in April 1803 as a result of the conditions of his imprisonment. He began a hero of the revolution to the Haitians and remains an inspiration to this day.

7.7 - Jean Jacques Dessalines

During 1802 it became clear that the French government did not intend to honour its commitment to the abolition of slavery. The institution was reintroduced on other French colonies such as Guadalupe and New Granada. This prompted an uprising by the former slaves of Saint Domingue. They had a taste of freedom and knew how easily it could be taken away unless they were united and mobilised.

First LeClerc, then his replacement the Comte de Rochambeau (LeClerc died of Yellow Fever towards the end of 1802) instigated brutal repression of the rebellion in an effort to remain in control. The reprisals they took against the rebels only served to unite them more fiercely against the French. To make matters worse, Napoleon was immersed in a large-scale conflict in Europe against the British, Prussians and Russians. He sold French possessions in Louisiana to the Americans in order to consolidate his forces in Europe. It seemed that Napoleon was too stretched to offer significant resources to the suppression of a rebellion in the Caribbean. The

British blockaded Saint Domingue's ports as part of their war against Napoleon which prevented re-supply and reinforcement of the French troops already there.

Meanwhile, the rebels had a new leader, Jean Jacques Dessalines. Dessalines was a black who had initially supported the French. He had been instrumental in the arrest of Louverture but by now had, like his predecessor, switched sides to wholly support the rebels. His troops had completely overrun the island isolating the French in a few northern ports. Dessalines won a decisive victory over the French troops at the city of Cap-Haitien in November 1803. Rochambeau surrendered to the British in December and his troops were given safe passage home.

On January 1st, 1804, Dessalines declared the island fully independent of France. He named the new nation Haiti, after a word in the language of the native Arawak people who had been driven to extinction by the Spanish. It meant 'land of high mountains'. Like Louverture before him, Dessalines promptly made himself a dictator of the new republic. He believed the only way to secure independence from white rule was to eliminate the whites entirely. Dessalines presided over a massacre of the entire, remaining white population of Haiti. Many whites and freed blacks fled Dessalines regime for Cuba or Louisiana. There was a deal of reluctance among his forces to carry out the orders and in many cases, they only happened before he was due to visit a particular town or city, or after he arrived and personally ordered the executions.

Men were executed first. Women were often raped before being killed. Children were also killed. Dessalines reasoning was that women would produce a new generation of whites to threaten Haitian freedom, children would grow up seeking revenge. In some cases he declared amnesty for a population to persuade them out of hiding, only to then kill them. Around five thousand people were murdered during Dessalines purge of Haiti's white population. His brutality was rewarded in 1806 when he was assassinated by one of his rivals for power.

7.8 – Aftermath

From its inception, the Haitian republic struggled to form a functioning state. Almost all of the ruling white elite, educated and skilled in running the cash crop economy of the island, had been murdered. Worse still, the 'gens de couleur' who were also educated and in many cases used to property ownership had been driven away by the outrages of Dessaline's regime. An overwhelming majority of the remaining Haitian population was illiterate and completely unqualified to revive the Haitian economy. This would certainly have harmed the credibility of the new Haitian government in the eyes of European nations and the United States, already accustomed to seeing blacks as inferior.

The fledgeling Haitian republic was not recognised by other nations and so unable to trade with them. Britain, France, Spain and the United States all had slave populations, either in colonies or within their country (as is the case with the United States). Britain would not abolish slavery for another thirty years and would have been afraid to recognize the Haitian republic for fear of the example that would set to other colonies with large slave populations. In Britain's case, Jamaica lay too close to Haiti to consider the possibility of helping Haiti to prosper. Racism would also have played it's part in the decision not to acknowledge the new regime, with white western nations taking the view that blacks simply could not organise sufficiently to effectively form the administration of a country.

In 1825, the French monarch Charles X wished to re-colonise Haiti. By this time, the days of the well organised Louverture army were long gone. With no economy to speak of it had not been possible for Haiti to maintain a military capable of taking on an imperial power. Haitian president Jean Pierre Boyer agreed to make reparation payments to France totalling 150 million francs. These payments continued for a century but were continued in order to forestall any attempts at re-colonisation. For a poor economy, these enforced payments were crippling and played a major part in keeping Haiti poor for generations to come.

The Haitian Revolution was viewed with almost universal horror around the major powers of the world. From the foundation of the first overseas colony utilising slave labour, there had always been a nightmare of the slave insurrection. This was born out of racist views on the savagery of black African natives, to which they might revert if freed from the bonds of slavery. The violence would have played into this fear. It was also born out of the horror of the implosion of lucrative cash crop economies to which Europe and American economies had become wholly dependent. The slave owners of the American south knew that their way of life depended on the institution of slavery in their economy. When this institution was taken away the south was lost forever. This was previewed for those slave owners in what became the Republic of Haiti.

First, they saw the abolition of slavery at the hands of a slave rebellion. They saw those former slaves overthrow the rule of colonial overlords in order to protest their freedom. Finally, and worst of all, they saw those former slaves committing horrific acts of cruelty and brutality against the white population in vengeance for their treatment. No slave owner in the world could read of these events without feeling fear for their own position, particularly in imperial colonies where the white population was dramatically outnumbered by the slave population.

Racism played a major part in the refusal to acknowledge Haiti. Governments which were completely made up of white men could not acknowledge a government composed of black former slaves. Many justified both slavery and colonialism by claiming that people of African descent were less human than those of European descent. To acknowledge the sovereignty of an entirely black nation would place it on the same level of Britain, France, Russia or the United States. That would undermine the justification for owning slaves (that they are sub-human and so not subject to the same rights as whites) and the owning colonies (the natives are in need of civilising by their more developed white overlords). These two concepts, slavery and colonialism were fundamental to the wealth and power of the European and American nations in the nineteenth century and this could not be put in jeopardy by recognising the sovereignty of Haiti.

In perpetrating his acts of violence, Dessaline made no attempt to cover them up. He saw his actions as a necessary step on the road to freedom and statehood for his country. He was keen for other nations to know that Haiti was not a country that sought to export it's revolutionary ideas to other slave colonies. But the massacre perpetrated at his orders and his personal insistence was too great an atrocity for any nation to overlook. It would have been hard enough for slave-owning nations to recognise Haiti, even if the revolution had been achieved completely peacefully. The terrible revenge taken on the white population, however, made it impossible.

All of these factors set the tone for Haiti's struggles through the nineteenth and twentieth century. The circumstances of the slave rebellion placed a millstone around the neck of the Haitian people that would keep them in poverty. Because of the failure of other nations to recognise Haiti, the Haitian economy never achieved the levels of wealth and prosperity they had achieved under the white rule. Through the nineteenth and twentieth centuries, there was a succession of coups and civil war while crime engulfed cities and towns.

The relatively recent Haitian earthquake produced a loss of life into the tens of thousands, both from the devastation wreaked on Haiti's slums and shanty towns but also from the disease that followed the breakdown of infrastructure in the aftermath. While natural disasters are often accompanied by large-scale loss of life the Haitian Revolution can claim the death toll from the Haitian earthquake. Had Haiti been an all-white colony it's economy may well have returned to prosperity after the revolution. Instead, it was a nation that struggled with poverty, poor infrastructure and chaotic governments for two hundred years. And so when natural disaster struck, the consequences were even more devastating.

But the Haitian Revolution has also been an inspiration across other nations of the world. As attitudes to race have changed, historians have reexamined the slave rebellion in Haiti and its impact on the Atlantic world (Europe and America). In Louisiana, the Haitian example inspired a slave rebellion. John Brown, the famous American abolitionist, also cited Haiti as an inspiration for his own work. While both resulted in violence and loss of life, they were also pivotal in the struggle for the abolition of slavery. John Brown's example served as an inspiration to many who sought to help slaves escape the South and would have inspired many educated Northerners to join the Union army during the American Civil War.

Karl Marx cited the Haitian Revolution as an example of a class war in which the workers overthrew the bourgeois ruling elite and took possession of the means of production. Marx would go on to inspire the Russians to overthrow the despotic and decadent Czars. While this too would precipitate bloodshed it also proved pivotal to twentieth-century history.

The first true leader of the Haitian revolution has also become a figure revered all over the world as a liberator. Toussaint Louverture was not tainted with the bloodshed of the massacre but is remembered for his leadership and his desire to ensure the freedom of his people, even when that meant going back to work in the fields for the French. Statues exist to him throughout the Americas, Cuba, Canada and even Paris.

CHAPTER 8

THE CUBAN REVOLUTION

Introduction

The Cuban Revolution saw the overthrow of General Fulgencio Batista, who himself had himself seized power in a military coup, after several years of armed struggle by the forces of Fidel Castro. Castro was a former lawyer who had been angered by Batista's abolition of elections after he had seized power and his co-operation in the exploitation of Cuban resources by American businesses. Castro survived imprisonment and exile from his own country and fought a guerrilla war against government forces from 1953 to 1959.

Having forced Batista to flee the country Castro declared himself 'President for Life', but crucially on a platform of acting for the people of Cuba. Castro was socialist in his political outlook, desiring to see Cuban resources in the hands of the Cuban people and not foreign companies. This led to him being snubbed by his most powerful neighbour, the United States, and drove Cuba in the welcoming arms of the Soviet Union. Cuba became an ally of the Soviets, a fact which would increase the tensions of the Cold War exponentially, due to Cuba's proximity to mainland America.

This tension would reach its peak during the Cuban Missile Crisis.

The expulsion of Batista and the rise of Castro's Communist dictatorship would have a profound effect on world politics for the next fifty years, bringing the world to the brink of nuclear disaster. This revolution was the last in a series of armed conflicts fought by Cubans against the rule and exploitation of foreign powers. The first significant series of conflicts occurred in the second half of the eighteenth century and resulted in both Cuban independence from Spain and its immediate annexation by the United States. These independence conflicts shifted the antagonists for the Cuban nationalists from the Spanish imperialists to the American capitalists. In turn, this would encourage the growth of socialist ideologies and the ultimate rejection of America and the West and alignment with the Soviet Union.

8.1 - The Ten Years War

Cuba had been colonised by the Spanish in the early sixteenth century, it's native peoples enslaved. The first settlement was founded by Diego Velazquez de Cuellar at Baracoa in 1511, followed by the settlement of San Cristobal de la Habana in 1515. This would become the capital, Havana. The dominant native population were the Taino, who were enslaved into the Spanish encomienda system. This was a feudal system by which the labour of native peoples conquered by the Spanish was granted to an individual in perpetuity by the Spanish Crown. By this means Spanish nobility became wealthy landowners with a ready-made slave workforce at their disposal.

Over the next three hundred years, it was largely ignored by the Spanish Empire, which was more concerned with exploiting the mineral wealth of their larger North American possessions. Cuba grew as an outpost of the Imperial administration rather than a cash crop agricultural economy. Towns and then cities flourished and the agriculture of the island was diverse, not the large-scale single crop plantation found in Jamaica or Saint Domingue, for example. In 1754 the Seven Years War broke out and Cuba found itself captured from the Spanish by the British. Trade with North America was opened up as the British sought to establish trade links with their other colonies. The biggest change the British brought about in Cuba, however, was the implementation of the single crop economy, in this case, sugar. They brought in huge numbers of slaves in order to produce and harvest large-scale sugar plantations.

The Seven Years War ended with the Peace of Paris, as part of which the British exchanged Cuba with the Spanish in exchange for Florida. By the end of the eighteenth century through the international situation was changing. Haiti, formerly half owned by the Spanish and a significant producer of sugar, won its independence in a bloody revolution. This was followed by similar rebellions in Spain's mainland territories. By the nineteenth century, the Spanish empire had refocused its imperial attention on a much smaller range of possessions. Cuba was at its heart. With Haiti shunned by the international community because of a combination of racism and fear of similar slave uprisings elsewhere, it's sugar was removed from the world market. As the century progressed, Cuban sugar would come to dominate the market and completely change the Cuban economy.

In 1817 the Cuban population was around 630,000 of which roughly half were white, around two hundred thousand were black slaves and about one hundred thousand were freed people of colour. This last social group was unique to Cuba, at least in such high numbers, and is a testament to the growing urban society in Cuba. Due to the proportion of Cuban slaves working in urbanised settings, there was a significantly high number of cases of 'coartacion' which translates literally as 'buying oneself out of slavery'. This would certainly not have been the case for other slave societies, such as Haiti or the Southern United States and appears to be peculiar to Cuba.

By the middle of the nineteenth century, Cuban sugar was the primary world source and a sugar boom gripped the Cuban economy. Spanish landowners scrambled to convert their lands to sugar production. The Cuban economy experienced a boom. Over a million African slaves were brought to Cuba in the nineteenth century to fuel the sugar boom. However, the benefits of the economic growth were not felt by Cuban nationals. Despite representing less than ten percent of Cuba's population, the Spanish controlled more than ninety percent of the island's wealth. Cuban nationals were given no representation in the Spanish parliament and were forced to pay taxes to the Spanish exchequer (echoing the plight of North American colonists a century earlier). In addition to this, the Spanish were jealously protective of the wealth which Cuba generated from them. The opposition was brutally repressed, the press and political opposition silenced.

In July 1867 the Revolutionary Committee of Bayamo was founded by a wealthy Cuban plantation owner named Francisco Vicente Aguilera. Bayamo was a town in the south-east of the island but the revolutionary conspiracy spread throughout eastern Cuba. In particular in Manzanillo under the leadership of Manuel de Cespedes. He led an uprising in 1868. It began on the 10th of October and by the end of the month, the movement had gained 12,000 followers throughout the east of the country. This was the beginning of what would become known as the Ten Years War. It was the first attempt to win independence by force.

On the 10th of April 1869, a constitutional assembly met and decided the form the government of the Cuban republic should take. Having decided on a constitution which separated civil government from the army and made the military subordinate to the elected leader, the Assembly became the House of Representatives and led by their first Cespedes, who was elected on April the 12th 1869.

The response of the Spanish government was brutal repression. Concentration camps were created and draconian laws put in place to control the population. Towns that refused to surrender were razed to the ground, Cuban nationals were forced to remain on their plantations or places of residence without sufficient reason could face summary execution.

The uprising of the Ten Years War would ultimately fail to secure independence for Cuba. Spain increased its troop's numbers and the revolutionary leaders themselves were either killed or became divided by political infighting. Crucially, they had failed to spread their revolutionary fervour to the wealthy western half of Cuba, where neither landowners nor slaves rose against the Spanish. The War ended in an effective stalemate with promises of reforms from Spain which did not materialise. Slavery was abolished in October 1886 but, accompanied by an economic depression, newly freed slaves found their wages too low to keep themselves out of poverty.

Though a failure, the Ten Years War had ignited the revolutionary spark which would ultimately lead to the defeat of the Spanish almost twenty years later

8.2 - The War of Independence

In the seventeen years between the Ten Years, War and the War of Independence Cuba changed significantly. With the abolition of slavery came radical changes to the Cuban economy. Smaller, Cuban owned, sugar mills were forced to close. Only the largest plantations and companies survived. This would feed into Cuban discontent. Cuba's cause was finding sympathy in the United States, where Cuban nationalists exiled from the island were publicising the independence cause. In the upper echelons of the American government, there was also a growing belief that the United States should be taking steps to annex Spanish possessions in the Americas;

neutralising the European influence in the western hemisphere and increasing the power of the United States over their Central and South American neighbours.

Jose Julian Marti Perez was the principal leader of the independence movement. He had been exiled to the United States following the Ten Years War and there, particularly in the state of Florida he worked to gather support and publicise the independence cause. This, in particular, was to prove a pivotal factor for Cubans. Their cause was seized upon by the journalists of the Hearst newspapers, who sensationalized the brutality of the Spanish and the heroism of the Cubans. Many Americans would have been moved by these accounts which resonated with their own relatively recent history. At the same time the intellectual and political elite of the United States were looking beyond their country's borders for the first time since its birth, believing that the vitality and energy that had covered the North American continent from coast to coast, and it was now their destiny to build an overseas mercantile empire in emulation of the British. So, the cause of Cuban nationalism was popular and seen as a first step in securing overseas territories for the United States.

The War of Independence began on February 25th, 1895 with uprisings across the island. Like the Ten Years War, these uprisings were initially confined to the east of the island. But an attempt by the Spanish to contain the revolutionaries failed and by January 22nd, 1896 they had reached the westernmost tip of the island. The Spanish fortified themselves into towns and cities, forcing the civilian population of western Cuba into these enclaves. In the overcrowded conditions and estimated 170,000 civilians died. The decisive moment for Cuba came when the United States dispatched the USS Maine to Havana to protect American citizens living there. On February 15th, 1898 the Maine exploded and sank with a loss of more than 200 American servicemen. The Hearst papers were leading a public outcry against the Spanish and calling for American intervention in Cuba. Congress passed a resolution authorising President McKinley to use any military force necessary to help Cuba win its independence, with a stipulation that it was to be truly independent and not annexed to the United States. War was declared on April 20th, 1898.

8.3 - The American Occupation and the rise of Batista

Following the defeat of the Spanish and the liberation of Cuba, the United States was able to make use of legal loopholes to exploit the Cuban economy. The agriculture of Cuba had already been transformed in favour of industrial-scale farming which only large companies could afford, driving smaller landholders out of business. Now US businesses began to dominate Cuba's exports. By the 1900's Americans owned more than ten percent of Cuban land and more than eighty percent of its ore exports. For the first thirty years of the twentieth century, America backed successive Cuban leaders and American troops were deployed more than once to protect American property and economic interests.

In 1933 the Sergeants Revolt brought a left-wing president to power, Ramon Grau. He instituted a Provisional Revolutionary government whose reforms led to the establishment of a large and prosperous Cuban middle class, the reform of land ownership and redistribution of wealth. Amongst other innovations was a ruling that half of all workforces in industry and agriculture had to be Cuban citizens (as opposed to immigrants), an eight-hour working day and votes for women. This government lasted around a year before being overthrown in a bloodless coup by a general named Fulgencio Batista. Batista was backed by the United States.

Ramon Grau would be re-elected as president in 1946, at this time a radical law student at the University of Havana made an impassioned speech against the president. It achieved notoriety enough to be covered by the local press. That firebrand was named Fidel Castro. The economic exploitation of Cuba by America had been the cause of his ire, and the corruption of the Grau regime. That ire would be stoked once again during the presidency of Batista leading to revolution.

After seizing power in 1934, Batista stood in free and fair elections and won in 1940 but was prevented from standing for a second term by the Cuban constitution. He would compete for the presidency again in 1952 however faced with almost certain defeat he seized power in another coup and abolished the elections.

It was in the 1952 elections that Fidel Castro was planning to stand for the Cuban Congress. The coup, followed by the effective abolition of democracy was a trigger for Castro, prompting him to begin planning to take power for himself.

Batista's time as president was characterised by economic prosperity for certain socio-economic groups in Cuba, particularly the middle classes. America was Cuba's biggest export market and was its largest source of imports. Middle-class Cuban's would vacation in Florida and purchase American luxury goods. There is evidence that Cuban ownership of automobiles and electrical goods was significantly greater than their Central and South American neighbours and, in fact, on a par with the developed European nations. But his government was rife with corruption and focused on American rather than Cuban interests.

It was this corruption, which lined the pockets of American companies and the Cuban elites to the disadvantage of Cuban working classes which so incensed Castro and his followers.

8.4 - Castro

Fidel Castro was born on August 13th, 1926. He studied law at the University of Havana and there discovered an interest in politics and became a political activist. Following his much-publicised attack on the

Grau government in 1946, he joined the Cuban People's Party in 1947 (the Partido Ortodoxo). This party had been created in response to widespread government corruption to promote Cuban national interests and implement social reforms. It included nationalists, communists and socialists. Members of the party were united by their desire to reform Cuban society and see it freed from its economic enslavement to the United States.

But Castro was not content simply to make speeches or participate in the democratic process. He was in favour of taking direct action to achieve his goals. This led to his involvement in an abortive attempt to overthrow the government of the Dominican Republic. This plan never got off the ground but by 1948 Castro was present in Colombia when a populist president, Jorge Eliecer Gaitan Ayala, was assassinated. Castro had admired the left wing president and took arms alongside his supporters in street riots that ensued, this included arming rioters with weapons stolen from police officers.

Upon his return to Cuba, Castro began practising law in a firm that provided legal representation to the poor and had planned to stand for political office in 1952. Fulgencio Batista seized power with the support of Cuban Communists but on taking control of the country he then abandoned his allies in favour of US capitalism. To Castro, Batista had not only cheated the Cuban people of their democracy but had abandoned his people in favour of American money, turning his back on socialism and Marxism. Politically, these were Castro's own beliefs, as demonstrated by his support for an assassinated socialist president in Colombia and his selfless decision to provide legal representation to the poor, even though he and his new wife were forced to rely on loans from family to make ends meet.

Castro founded a group which he called 'The Movement' in the summer of 1952. This consisted of intellectuals, farmers and factory workers from across Cuban society, all radicalised by their dissatisfaction with the status quo. Their first act was to attack an army barracks on July 26th, 1953. It was a failure in which most of the men Castro had recruited failed to arrive. Those that did were outgunned and outnumbered. They fled to the Sierra Maestra Mountains. It was there that they would be cornered and arrested by Batista's forces on August 1st, 1953.

Castro himself escaped summary execution and won many supporters as he eloquently defended himself in open court against a charge of attempting to overthrow and the Cuban government and constitution. He would subsequently be found guilty and sentenced to fifteen years in prison.

In 1955, Batista fought and won an election to become the legitimate president of Cuba and, deeming Castro no longer a populist threat, had him released on May 15th, 1955. Castro would return to his political activism, giving interviews on radio and to the press. He would be vocally critical of the Batista government, despite close monitoring and amid increasing crackdowns on demonstrators and political opponents. Later that year Castro would flee Cuba for Mexico.

8.5 - Castro and the Revolution

It was during his Mexican exile that Castro met and befriended an Argentinian doctor named Che Guevara. The two found they shared political values as well as a hatred of the United States. Guevara would become instrumental in Castro's Cuban revolution. Castro would go to spend five months raising funds from Cuban, anti-Batista emigres in the United States. He promised the overthrow of the Batista government, economic and social reform as well as economic freedom for Cuba.

In 1956 he returned to Cuba along with 81 volunteers. Upon landing in Cuba on December 2nd, 1956, Castro's men were overwhelmed by Batista's army and scattered into the mountains. From there Castro's forces began a campaign of guerrilla war against the army which culminated in the seizure of the military base of La Plata in January 1957 and with it control of the region. He secured the support of the local population by executing the local landlord of the area, a man despised by the populace. Anti-Batista sentiment was now breaking out throughout the country with riots breaking out in many cities and towns.

Castro knew that military success alone would not be sufficient. Just as Cuban nationalists had stoked American public opinion against Spain, so Castro sought to do the same in his cause. In February 1957 he made contact with Herbert Matthews of the New York Times. The interview would be read worldwide and would be the reason that the Cuban revolution became known outside of Cuba.

By 1958 Castro was gaining increasing momentum. As increasing numbers of anti-Batista Cuban exiles in the United States began to support Castro so the pressure grew on the US State Department. While the United States refused to directly intervene they decided to cease all military and financial support to the Batista regime. In desperation, the government launched an offensive on June 28th, 1958 in which a force twelve hundred strong was launched against Castro's Sierra Maestra headquarters. The attack was repulsed by forces commanded by Che Guevara.

This defeat left Castro in control of southeastern Cuba while the remains of Batista's army were besieged in the city of Santiago. This was enough for the United States to intervene. They employed Eulogio Cantillo to remove Batista from power. He engineered a ceasefire on the promise that Batista would be tried for war crimes. Instead, he allowed the president to flee the country with three hundred million dollars. A new president was briefly set up in his place, Carlos Piedra. But when Castro heard of the treachery he marched on Havana, arriving on January 2nd, 1959. Piedra was deposed and Cantillo sentenced to fifteen years in prison.

8.6 - Castro's Cuba

Initially, after the overthrow of Batista, Castro claimed no ambitions for the presidency of Cuba. Instead, he appointed Manuel Urrutia Lleo to the post. Urrutia was a lawyer who had been instrumental in persuading the American government to stop their support for Batista. He was also a liberal and more likely to gain American support than Castro, a guerrilla fighter. The presidency of Urrutia didn't last long. Castro overruled him on his decisions, such as his desire to shut down brothels and casinos which Castro opposed on the grounds that they were sources of employment. Castro was appointed Prime Minister on February 16th, 1959 but was increasingly acting as president in all but name. Urrutia resigned on July 18th.

Castro made a trip to the United States to establish how his new regime would be received. He met with Vice President Richard Nixon (VP to President Eisenhower) where he was confronted with CIA files detailing the communist links of many of his associates. Nixon's concern was that Castro was himself a Communist and that he planned to make Cuba into a Soviet satellite. Castro does not appear to have allayed any fears during his 1959 visit to the US, leading Nixon to conclude that either he was a Communist or he was simply ignorant of the Communist sympathisers that were rife in his country. The end result for the United States was the same; Castro had to be removed.

As Nixon was drawing up plans for a Cuban invasion (plans which would be halted temporarily by his defeat in the 1960 Presidential election) Castro was undertaking radical and widespread reform in his country. Any landowner who owned more than 1,000 acres had part of their lands seized and redistributed. This reform helped the impoverished and exploited Cuban peasants but would have confirmed the worst fears of the American government. This was the beginning of what would be a decades-long antipathy between America and Cuba, and the start of Cuba's drift into the orbit of the Soviet Union. Diplomatic relations between the United States and Cuba were officially severed in January 1961.

While the United States had cut off their ties to Cuba, Castro had yet to openly side with the Soviet Union, or admit to a Communist political ideology. This changed on April 17th, 1961 when around 1,500 CIA trained Cubans landed in the Bay of Pigs. Their intention of joining counter-revolutionary rebels who were fighting a guerrilla war against Castro. The mission was a disaster. The United States had been warned that the Soviet Union intended to give any and all support they could to Cuba if America acted openly. As a result, the new president John Kennedy could give no support to the doomed mission. The men found themselves under air attack from the Cuban air force and within forty-eight hours were all either killed or captured.

Almost two years later America would offer fifty million dollars worth of food and medical supplies to Cuba in exchange for the return of the Bay of Pigs survivors. Castro had defeated an attempt at regime change in Cuba and had won a pivotal public relations victory at the same time. The United States had been shown to be defeated. Castro now had the public support to openly renounce America and declare his allegiance to communism. The rebellion against Castro came to nothing, his rule was now secure and backed by one of the world's only two superpowers. The revolution was now complete.

8.7 - Aftermath

The immediate consequence of Castro's embracing of communism was the Cuban Missile Crisis. In response to the failed Bay of Pigs invasion and in retaliation for the deployment of American missiles in Italy and Turkey, Soviet Premier Nikita Khrushchev agreed to deploy nuclear missiles in Cuba. This had been requested by Castro to deter the United States from attempting another invasion. Construction on short and medium-range ballistic missile sites in Cuba began in the summer of 1962. The deployment was discovered by the Americans in 1962, following an overflight by a U2 spy plane, which photographed the missile sites under construction

President Kennedy implemented an immediate blockade of Cuba in order to prevent any further weapons from reaching the island. The United States threatened to attack Russia if Castro launched the missiles he had been given. What followed was a period of twelve days in October 1962 while America and Russia both sought to avert a nuclear holocaust through back channels. It was the closest the world had come to nuclear war between the United States and the Soviet Union, and the proximity of a communist state so close to the US mainland was the trigger for it.

Part of the negotiations that saw Russia remove the missiles from Cuba was a guarantee of Cuban sovereignty, with no further American backed attempts to overthrow Castro. This cemented Castro's revolution, leaving him secure to crush any domestic political opponents, and secure in his rule provided he remained in the orbit of the Soviets.

He would subsequently visit the Soviet Union In May 1963 where he was hailed as a hero. He would return to Cuba, newly invigorated with ideas to eliminate his last critics at home and make his rule more effective. Castro's government cracked down on religious ministers, labelling them as counter-revolutionary. He also allowed a brief window of emigration from Cuba and thus rid himself of a vocal and disapproving middle class.

But Castro was not content with the strengthening of his own regime. He believed the United States would continue to attempt to oust him, and there is some evidence that he was right. There were assassination attempts, all of which failed and theories that some or all were orchestrated by the CIA. But despite a growing military, Castro could not strike at the one country whom he saw as his greatest enemy. Instead, he sought to foment communist revolutions in other Central and South American countries. These included Chile, Argentina and Bolivia. His chief lieutenant, Che Guevara was in charge of these revolutionary movements. These South American campaigns were known as the 'Andean Project'. Castro also welcomed various left-leaning paramilitary groups to Cuba to carry out training. These included; the Black Panthers and the Viet Cong. Africa was another place rife with potential and actual revolutionary movements and Castro was at his most assiduous in offering Cuban support to various movements. These included supporting a socialist Algerian regime and a socialist movement in the Congo. In 1966 Castro staged a Tri-Continental Conference of Africa, Asia and Latin America. From this came the Latin American Solidarity Organisation whose mission statement was that the duty of any revolution was to ferment further revolution.

Castro wished to create a league of revolutionary regimes in countries newly freed from colonial ownership, an alliance which would raise Cuba to equal status alongside the United States and free him from his reliance on the goodwill of the Soviet Union. The military expeditions undertaken were generally unsuccessful and cost an estimated twenty thousand Cuban lives. In Bolivia, it would eventually take the life of Castro's charismatic and iconic fellow revolutionary when Guevara was tracked down and killed by government forces.

Under Batista, the Cuban economy had flourished. It was entirely reliant on the United States who exercised a great deal of economic and political control. Despite this many Cubans found themselves prospering. Cuba boasted respectable education and healthcare systems. Castro's revolution redressed the inequality of this wealth by redistributing land fairly among the peasant classes and ending the monopoly of American business over the Cuban economy. However, his communist inspired ideology meant that a relationship with America was impossible. As a result, Cuba was ostracised, unable to sell goods to anyone except the Soviets. In 1968, inspired by China's Great Leap Forward, Castro instigated the seizure of any remaining private property in Cuba. Now operating under an entirely state-owned economy, any motivation to increase productivity by the Cuban people, had disappeared. Castro's Great Revolutionary Offence began the decline of the Cuban economy.

After Castro's rise, Cuba found itself just as beholden to the Soviets as it had been to the Americans. As the economy began to collapse and living conditions to deteriorate through the 1970's and '80's and tens of thousands of Cubans attempted to flee to America. Thousands died attempting the crossing. When the Soviet Union dissolved, the Cuban economy crumbled further. Thousands more Cubans died of famine during the 1990's, until American food aid began to be accepted in 1993.

Castro did succeed in freeing his country from American exploitation but in so doing he condemned it to decades of isolation as a pariah state. While his social and political reforms were doubtless well-intentioned they were outweighed by the suffering of the Cuban people at the hands of the American trade embargo and the collapse of the power bloc upon which Castro had placed all of his hopes, the Soviet Union. Attempts to export the Cuban Revolution ultimately failed, though not without costing more Cuban lives.

One final legacy of Castro's revolutionary government was to come in the 2000's. No longer sending Cuban troops abroad to ferment socialist revolution, Castro agreed to send 20,000 trained doctors to Venezuela in exchange for oil. This arrangement proved successful and was later increased to 40,000 doctors in exchange for 100,000 oil barrels per day. Since the Cold War, Cuba has faded into obscurity but has remained a Communist state. Fidel Castro stood down as president in favour of his brother Raul on July 31st, 2006 but the communist ideology continued. Despite the embargoes and bitter economic hardship, Cuba continued its defiance towards the United States. Raul Castro publicly supported North Korea and just as publicly refused an audience with President Barack Obama, instead, he presented him with an open letter in a Havana newspaper, castigating the imperialist United States.

CHAPTER 9

THE TAIPING REVOLUTION

Introduction

The Taiping rebellion was a conflict fought in China between 1850 and 1864 between the ruling Qing dynasty and the Taiping Heavenly Kingdom. The rebellion began with the state persecution of a Christian sect known as the God Worshipping Society, which was led by Hong Xiuquan. Xiuquan believed himself to be the younger brother of Jesus Christ. The objectives of the Taiping rebels was the overthrow of the ruling Manchu dynasty and the implementation of their own version of Christianity as the official state religion of China. They wished not merely to supplant the ruling elite and bring about social reform, but to overturn every aspect of Chinese moral and political life. This included allowing social mobility for all by giving access to the Imperial civil service examinations to any who wished to apply as well as land and wealth redistribution policies that presaged the Communist revolution of the twentieth century

The death toll from the fourteen years of conflict is one which is unparalleled in human history with millions displaced and estimated casualties that range from twenty as high as one hundred million people.

9.1 - China in the mid-19th century

The origins of the Taiping rebellion and subsequent civil war lay in the decline of the ruling Qing dynasty. The Qing dynasty had its origins in Manchuria and elevated those of Manchu ethnicity above other ethnic groups. It was an imperial government by an ethnic minority which maintained strict controls over social mobility and controlled a large population of the impoverished and powerless peasantry. The Qing's governed China from the seventeenth century and brought about many economic revolutions of Chinese societies. But by the middle of the nineteenth century, the administration suffered from rampant corruption, with government offices being sold to the highest bidder. Those rich enough to purchase offices then used their position to monopolise community resources such as granaries.

The Qing dynasty's position of power was undermined by the increasing contact with foreign powers. Initially, when the first European traders had arrived, China had adopted the 'Canton system' whereby foreigners were only allowed to land and trade at the port of Canton (now Guangzhou). By the 1790's nations such as Britain were becoming concerned at the one-sided nature of trade with China. There were many Chinese goods which were in demand in Europe, such as tea, silk and ceramics. However, the Chinese economy was largely self-sufficient and there was nothing they needed from the Westerners. Consequently, the only trade possible was in silver, meaning an increasing amount of finite Western silver stocks were being funnelled into China for its export commodities.

The only product which was in demand for import into China was opium. To meet this demand the British East India Company had been significantly increasing its opium production in India. The Daoguang Emperor, increasingly concerned over the amount of opium his people were consuming, both in terms of the cost and the health risks, decided to ban the import of opium. This action sparked two wars with the British, the

Opium Wars, at the end of the nineteenth century. The result was a complete humiliation for China at the hands of a technologically superior European force. The Qing government was forced to open up other port cities in addition to Canton to Western merchants and Christian missionaries. Those foreigners who were now allowed much greater access to China were also subject to their own laws, often completely outside of Chinese jurisdiction no matter what crimes they committed. It was the defeat in the First Opium War that led to the surrender of Hong Kong island to the British in perpetuity.

Prior to this, the Qing dynasty had held itself and the Chinese state as a significant power in the region and probably more than a match for the Western powers that had sought its trade. Those powers, after all, had accepted Chinese conditions on their merchants and accepted an unequal trading relationship that saw Western silver enrich the Imperial coffers in order to meet the demand for Chinese goods. The Qing court was given a short, sharp lesson in how far behind the Western powers China had actually fallen. The Imperial Navy consisted of wooden sailing junks, which had been hopelessly outclassed by the Royal Navy. British troops had been armed with modern muskets and artillery, easily defeating Imperial forces on the ground. When the Qing emperor was forced to accept all conditions imposed on China including the payment of reparations to the victors this, in turn, led to rebellions within China. The Manchu Chinese that comprised the Qing dynasty and the Imperial elite was already despised by the Han ethnic majority that made up China. As a result, any sign of weakness in the ruling Manchu dynasty was an invitation to revolt.

In combination with this political and military defeat, a series of bad harvests led to famine in northern China and widespread movement of population to the south. This, in turn, led to overpopulation problems in an already densely populated region. Law and order began to break down and banditry was rife. There was widespread discontent among the impoverished and increasingly pressured peasantry for whom there seemed no relief from natural and man-made travails. Traditional Chinese religious belief is in a pantheon of utilitarian gods who bestow blessings on those who show them honour. These gods would be favoured when it was seen that the giving of gifts such as incense resulted in rewards, such as a good harvest. When this did not happen, no matter the scale of the gifts, the gods would be abandoned in favour of others.

As the traditional Chinese gods seemed unable to help their follower it resulted in a spiritual vacuum which Christianity was able to fill. The pragmatic Chinese had seen how completely the Europeans had been able to defeat the mighty Imperial Qing army and navy and reasoned that this power and superiority stemmed from their morality and their religion. This was the way of Chinese thinking. So, there was an increasing willingness to accept the European God, as his native followers were clearly benefiting greatly from their worship.

China was an agrarian society at this time and as such vulnerable to anything which may impact on the health of their crops. During the nineteenth century, this agricultural society saw a shift from the small farmer to the large landowner. Increasingly, only the larger landowners could produce more than a subsistence living from the land. China was a land of inequality, wealth and property were concentrated in the hands of a minority. Political power was concentrated in the hands of an ethnic minority, the Manchu ruling elite, despite the majority of Chinese people being of Han ethnicity.

The inequalities of Chinese society were exacerbated by the intrusion of foreign powers into the Chinese economy. The arrival of the British, with their desire for an opium trade, resulted in two wars in which the Qing dynasty was humbled and forced to accept humiliating terms. Foreign mercantile influence then began to impact the Chinese currency, as their exploitation led to the funnelling of wealth from the Manchu elite and into the coffers of the British East India Company and others. China was left the poorer and it's currency devalued. This, in turn, led to price inflation which would further widen the growing gap between rich and poor.

It was into this environment of discontent and suffering, with a dissatisfaction in both the secular government and the traditional gods that a messiah appeared who would be the catalyst for a revolution. That Messiah was a man named Hong Houxiu.

9.2 - Hong Houxiu

He was born near the city of Canton in southern China. He displayed an aptitude for the scholarly arts at an early age so his family made financial sacrifices in order to provide him with a formal education. He began his education at a local primary school at the age of five. He placed first in the local civil service preliminary examinations and by the age of sixteen was ready to attempt the prefectural examinations which would have allowed him admission to the scholar-bureaucrat class of the imperial civil service. This was the traditional route of advancement for many young Chinese men which involved developing an expertise in literature and philosophy to prove worthiness to hold public office. Hong would attempt the examination three times between 1827 and 1836 and would fail each time.

It was during this time that he encountered a Christian preacher in the streets of Canton and accepted some literature from the man out of curiosity. When he failed his exam for the third time he fell into a depression and experienced a mental and physical breakdown. He was bedridden for forty days and while incapacitated experienced a series of visions. In these visions, it was revealed to him that the ruling Qing dynasty were in fact demons. He saw himself singled out to destroy the demons and bring China back to the true God. When he awoke he began to study the Christian literature he had been given and came to the conclusion that the vision had been given to him by the God of Christianity, and that it was his mission to restore China to this true faith.

This realisation came over a period of six years, during which he worked as a teacher and attempted the examinations one more time, only to fail. In 1847 he would spend time studying with an American missionary in Canton named Issachar Roberts, and would eventually baptise himself into the Christian faith. During the vision, God had told him that he may take the name Xiuquan, which meant Accomplished and Perfect. Hong Xiuquan was thus born.

He began his evangelising by converting members of his family, notably his cousin Feng Yunshan. He and his followers became notorious as iconoclasts, destroying idols of the Chinese gods and vandalising their temples. Eventually, this practice would lead to their expulsion from local towns at the hands of the gentry. They fled to the remote mountainous area of the Guangxi region of southwestern China. At Thistle Mountain, they would set up their headquarters. The movement named themselves the God-Worshippers and their numbers soon swelled to more than three thousand. They were popular with the Chinese peasantry because they provided; stability through the raising of a militia to protect the faithful from bandits; and social security, by raising funds from their members to help those in need.

At this time, even geographically remote areas of China comprised a dense network of interconnected villages. These communities were connected by the shared maintenance of paddy fields as well as community inter-trade routes. As a result, even the remotest village would have received news and rumours, spread by word of mouth, of the powerful Westerners who had established themselves along the coast and inflicted such defeats on the emperor. To many, the opportunity to join a faith which had bestowed such strength was an attractive proposition.

9.3 - Civil War

As the popularity of the God Worshippers grew Xiuquan adopted the town of Qingtian, which lay near to Thistle Mountain, as the headquarters for his followers. It was in Qingtian that the rebellion would first appear. Increasingly concerned about the breakdown of law and order in Guangxi province, as well as the stories of the God Worshippers cult and their practice of icon and temple destruction, the imperial government sent troops to investigate. They attempted to capture Qingtian but were resisted and subsequently defeated by Xiuquan forces on the January 11th, 1851.

The God Worshippers fought their way along the Yangtze River and eventually captured the city of Nanjing. This would become the capital of a new kingdom, with Xiuquan as it's King. Xiuquan subsequently declared himself the Heavenly King and announced the formation of the Taiping, or the Heavenly Kingdom. The movement had gone from a group of Christian converts intent on demolishing the symbols of other, false, gods to a self-declared nation in direct opposition to imperial China and it's Qing rulers. According to stories, as Xiuquan believed that the Manchu were demons when Nanjing was captured all of the Manchu men were executed while the women were forced out of the city and then burned alive. Such stories tend to proliferate when one side in a conflict professes some kind of religious crusade and stories like this may well be part of Qing propaganda against the Taiping rebels.

Propaganda of this kind may well have been a necessary part of the fight for the Qing dynasty given that the Taiping political and social agenda would have made them popular with the ordinary Chinese peasantry. The proposed land reform and the redistribution of wealth, which would have meant that the long-suffering peasant classes welcomed the forces of the Heavenly Kingdom with open arms. It was also a reason for the Taiping's ability to recruit to their banner. The forces which the Heavenly Kingdom were able to field was more than a match for anything the Qing dynasty could muster in terms of manpower. In contrast, there was a great deal of resistance to Taiping ideology among the landowning middle classes, who tended to be traditionalist and conservative. While the loyalty of the peasant classes meant a ready supply of soldiers, the failure to persuade any of the social elites meant that the revolt remained a grassroots movement, without political support from any group that may be able to influence the Qing court.

Shortly after the capture of Nanjing, the Taiping army launched further campaigns in the north and west. Their intention was to rapidly expand the territory of the Heavenly Kingdom but these campaigns proved unsuccessful. There was now in-fighting among the Taiping leadership, with Xiuquan becoming paranoid and ordering a series of assassinations of those he believed to be plotting against him.

Following the capture of Nanjing, the Taiping army laid siege to the city of Changsha in the Hunan province, south of the Yangzi River. Capture of this city would bring with it the fall of a wealthy province. The imperial government asked a senior official named Zeng Guofan to suppress the unrest in the Hunan province. He was offered the rank of Chief of Staff and given the authority to raise an army to deal with the uprising. Guofan was of Han ethnicity. The Han had ruled China to the south of the Great Wall until they had been conquered by the Manchu, whose homelands were north of the wall. Since then the Manchu's had controlled the most important offices of state. Ethnic resentment against the Manchu's was one of the battle cries of the rebellion. The Taiping rebels were ethnic Hans, wanting to overturn the Manchu Confucian system entirely. As they advanced eastwards from their new capital so other Han rebels arose to further weaken imperial control.

So far, the Taiping army had enjoyed great success on the battlefield, against Manchu soldiers. The garrisons of Nanjing and Hangzhou were wiped out to a man, Manchu's all. The ethnic Han, Taiping army appeared more than a match for the Manchu imperial forces. By making Zeng the Chief of Staff the emperor hoped to match Han against Han. Zeng would raise an army of Han with which to fight the Taiping hordes. In this, he was to prove ultimately successful, though only after years of constant warfare.

Upon being appointed to his new position, Zeng set about securing the province against the Han rebellions that had erupted in anticipation of the Taiping invasion. His methods were brutal and resulted in the executions of tens of thousands of people. He also enforced a policy of conscription, requiring at least one male from every household to be available for the draft. While the Taiping rebels appealed to the lowest members of Chinese society with their policy of redistributing wealth and property, Zeng took the opposite approach. He appealed to the wealthy, ethnic Han, land-owning gentry.

He was also given extensive powers to fund the army he was building, which was achieved by devolving tax-raising powers to the province. This was the beginning of a policy of devolution of power from a central authority to the local level. Zeng could also sell political offices, which allowed local Han landowners to buy their way into an Imperial bureaucracy which otherwise would have been closed to them. All of this devolution of power would be significant for China moving into the 20th century. It would bring about the downfall of the Qing dynasty, the Confucian system and imperial China altogether.

By the summer of 1854, the Taiping army had been repulsed from Hunan province by Zeng's army. The two forces would then battle each other up and down the Yangtze River for the next decade, taking and retaking the same villages and towns. The Hunan army wrought a great deal of destruction in its practice of a scorched earth strategy in order to deny shelter or supplies to the Taiping, where the Hunan army was forced into retreat. This policy contributed greatly to the death toll of the conflict as it led inevitably to famine and disease.

The makeup of these opposing forces represents the conflict as a whole. The Taipings were a religious movement, fighting to free China from the rule of demons and restore, so they believed Christianity. They stood for taking wealth from the social and political elites and re-distributing it. Later Chinese Communists would describe the Taiping as Proto-Communists.

In contrast, they were opposed by a force who had been forcibly conscripted and paid for by the wealthy elite. The Hunan army of Zeng Guofan fought to defend the agnostic Confucian system that had been the backbone of imperial government for centuries. They represented a secular state which held the arts above the sciences and saw religion as a matter of everyday pragmatism rather than as the core of a moral code. It was a battle between the tradition and innovation, between those with a vested interest in the status quo and those who had suffered under Confucianism for generations, who now had a voice and a means of bettering themselves on the physical plane as well as the spiritual.

9.4 - Defeat of the Taiping Uprising

An attempt by the Taiping rebels to capture Shanghai was defeated in 1860 by a Qing army supported by European officers led by Frederick Townsend Ward. This army would become known as the 'Ever Victorious Army' under another European, Charles George Gordon and would be instrumental in the eventual defeat of the Taiping. Gordon's Qing troops defeated another Shanghai attack in 1862 and successfully defended a number of treaty ports (ports which it had been agreed Westerners could trade through) such as Ningbo. For the Taiping to capture one of these ports would have been a crucial victory, providing the Heavenly Kingdom with the opportunity to deal directly with representatives from Western powers, and potentially negotiate as a legitimate state. However, the Western powers felt threatened by the radical nature of the Taiping policies and the violence they had instigated with their rebellion. Their only wish was to restore order so that their trade would be uninterrupted.

The European led 'Ever Victorious Army' was then deployed to support Imperial troops in ousting the rebels from key strongholds along the Yangtze River. Imperial Qing forces were reorganised for the Yangtze campaign under three generals; Zeng Guofan, Zuo Zongtang and Li Hongzhang. In particular, Guofan organised his forces in the Hunan province where he raised a peasant army. By 1864 Qing control in most areas had been re-established.

Central China was left a devastated region. The campaigns had raged backwards and forwards over the same territory for almost a decade and had become a campaign of total war. This meant that any and all civilian infrastructure and resources were considered to be viable targets. The death toll rose into the tens of millions whether as a result of war or the famine and disease that was the inevitable result of such widespread economic destruction.

Hong Xiuquan fell ill with food poisoning in 1864 during the final siege of Nanjing, the last Taiping stronghold. He died twenty days later. Before his death, he abdicated his throne in favour of his fifteen-year-old son. But by this time the Heavenly Kingdom was no more. Allow the fall of Nanjing and the death of Xiuquan marked the official end of the Taiping rebellion there were still hundreds of thousands of Taiping troops at large, scattered throughout different provinces. It was not until August 1871 that the last Taiping army was defeated and the war was officially over.

Even when the Taiping rebels had finally been suppressed the Qing dynasty found it lacked the strength to hold it's territory securely. A series of other ethnic uprisings occurred, as other groups sought to take advantage of perceived Qing weakness to try and forge their own lands out of the Empire. The Nian Rebellion (1853 - 68), and rebellions by Chinese Muslims were just a few of the conflicts which continued to break out.

9.5 - Taiping beliefs

The Taiping were undoubtedly responsible for unleashing one of the bloodiest conflicts in human history. There are accounts of appalling brutality when towns and villages were taken, such as the slaughter of Manchu men and the burning alive of Manchu women, believing the Manchu to be demons. Certainly, Xiuquan displayed an intolerance of any but his own specific belief system when he and his early followers set about destroying idols and defacing temples. However, the Taipings were not as alien to the ordinary Confucian Chinese as they first appear to be. This may explain the popularity of their movement.

They preached strict adherence to marriage and monogamy but following the capture of Nanjing quickly abandoned these views and returned to the practice of polygamy. Temples and idols were destroyed, when the Taiping became aware of them. But temple attendants were not tortured or killed, merely sent away. In fact, many temples had been allowed to fall into a state of dilapidation before the Taiping arrived, as the local populace had more pressing demands on their purse and time. Much of the tearing down of the relics of the old gods took place to the ambivalence of the locals.

9.6 - Religious Zeal

The Taipings were not alone in their religious zeal, other rebellions against the Qing regime sprang into being on the back of the chaos caused by the Taiping-Qing conflict. These included Buddhists, Daoists and Muslims who allied themselves with and were even absorbed into the Taiping military machine. At its peak, the Taiping army numbered hundreds of thousands. While there seems no doubt as to the zealotry of the founding core, and probably not the upper echelons of the officer class there would have been many under the Taiping banner who did not share

Xiuquan faith. This would have included those peasants who saw a better life for themselves under the Taiping rule than the Qing dynasty, moderates who shared some of Xiuquan beliefs but not to such extremes and those who merely sought to fight the Qing. In this way, many of the Taiping revolutionaries were still pragmatic Chinese Confucians in their way of thinking.

However, there is no question that the belief in a monotheistic god complete with the full accoutrements of ritual, holy text and ceremony. While Confucianism had its share of ritual and belief, it was a philosophy in which the gods could be discarded if they proved ineffective. Taiping was revolutionary in their belief in an all-powerful deity with control over human destiny.

9.7 - Women

One aspect of Taiping belief which differed radically from Chinese tradition was their attitude towards women. Xiuquan gave women equal status to men in the Heavenly Kingdom. He went further in allowing women access to formal education and to take part in imperial examinations. They also took arms and fought alongside the men. The Taiping did practice strict segregation of the sexes which further supported their independence by freeing them of any dependence on men.

This revolutionary attitude was later dropped after the taking of Nanjing, with a return to the traditional practice of polygamy and the status of women as possessions. However, this is linked to the fact that the Taiping's remarkable success was partly due to the enormous numbers of recruits they were able to draw on. And as has already been discussed, not all of these recruits shared the lofty ideals of Hong Xiuquan. The reversal on the policy of intermingling of the sexes may well have been to prevent discontent and mass desertion within the army ranks. The return to more traditional Chinese beliefs may also have been part of a strategic decision to make the Heavenly Kingdom more attractive and less alien to the mass of the Chinese populace, in a bid to garner more support among the upper classes.

9.8 - Democracy

There is evidence that Hong Xiuquan believed in a universal suffrage, in the concept of all people being equal across political, religious, racial and gender lines. He also believed that everyone should have access to the imperial examinations. Under the previous emperors, numerous groups were barred from the examinations whether on the basis of ethnicity, profession or gender. Even the position of Emperor was to be democratized. Under the Confucian system the Emperor as a mystical, semi-deified being. The Taiping regarded the title of Emperor as just that, a title alone. This was sacrilegious but part of their belief in the universal suffrage of all men and women and the democratic ideal.

9.9 - Aftermath

There are two principal legacies of the Taiping revolution. The economy of Central China was thrown into disarray because of the destruction wrought on communities fought over for a decade. Some towns and villages changed hands several times during the course of the conflict. The loss of life from the sustained fighting between Taiping and Qing forces is staggering whether in comparison to contemporary conflicts or the modern era. This, in turn, will have had an impact on the region for generations to come. The war was a total war, not limited simply to combatants and military targets. Both sides targeted civilians as both sides were seeking to stamp out the other's way of life. In the case of the Heavenly Kingdom, the war was a crusade against demons, with all the associated brutality and zealotry which one would expect from an army led by a religious fanatic who believed he was facing supernatural beings. For the Qing dynasty, the war was a defence of ancient Chinese traditions. The Taiping would burn down this society in favour of their own model and the Imperial forces were seeking to prevent that, by eliminating the communities who professed to be part of the Heavenly Kingdom if required.

As a result of the total nature of the conflict, the crusading element of the war (particularly for the Taiping forces) and the protracted nature of the fighting the consequences would be felt for a very long time. This would particularly be the case in regions of Central China which had been fought over so hard. Though the Taiping movement was ultimately defeated it would not be possible to forget for a long time. The Qing dynasty would not forget, nor would it be allowed to. The Taiping rebellion was not the last it would be faced with. The speed with which the Taiping had gathered its numbers and the territory it had been able to capture in such a short space of time will have been a lesson to all the disgruntled social and political groups in China seeking change. The Qing dynasty was not invulnerable. The Westerners had proved that the Imperial forces could be beaten and had demonstrated just how much more powerful their modern states were compared to the traditionalist Chinese nation. The example of the Taiping would inspire future revolutionaries.

The Taipings also introduced to those who either joined their ranks, or simply lived within the territory which they had captured, revolutionary concepts of universal suffrage, and freedom. They didn't practice democracy of politics, in which every individual has an input into the process of government. Rather they practised freedom of prayer. Each individual could not have their own personal connection to their god, not just the Emperor. They allowed the freedom of social mobility, opening the imperial examinations to all and thus promoting a true meritocracy. Once introduced those ideas would not be the easiest to disperse. Many ordinary Chinese will have returned to their former way of life, after the defeat of the Heavenly Kingdom, accepting the restrictions of Imperial life again. But some will have remembered the revolutionary concepts that gave them the freedom to practice their own religion, that gave them to improve their lot by giving them the possibility of upward social mobility. In the extreme poverty that would have faced many devastated communities these ideas will have resonated strongly and found fertile ground when other revolutionaries began calling for change and modernisation.

The Taiping introduced the concepts of wealth redistribution and land reform which would be revived a century later by Mao and the Communist revolutionaries. Though the Taiping were ultimately defeated, and the Qing dynasty attempted to erase all memory of them, they left behind them a far-reaching legacy which would have been passed on through word of mouth through those who survived the war. How many Chinese peasants whispered to themselves of the Heavenly Kingdom where every man was equal and the peasants had as much claim to the land as the nobility. It seems inevitable that some remnant of the Taiping philosophy would have been remembered. A century later those ideas would resurface in a revolution that would prove more successful than that of Hong Xiuquan.

CHAPTER 10

THE CHINESE REVOLUTIONS

Introduction

The twentieth century saw China transformed. The bloody Taiping rebellion was followed by increased foreign intervention to put down the Boxer Rebellion, with China forced to accept a peace treaty that was weighted heavily in favour of the foreign nations who sought to exploit it. The Qing dynasty brutally repressed any suggestion of political opposition and this drove those who sought reform overseas.

A new generation of young radicals had grown up, receiving university educations in foreign universities. They formed political parties and campaigned for reform and modernisation at home. The old order of the Manchu, Qing dynasty found itself under increasing pressure from these groups to change but the imperial court was still controlled by ultra-conservatives who consistently blocked reform attempts. Denied the meaningful change they wanted, the young radicals had only one avenue left, revolution.

Uprisings sprang up across China in the 1900's. Their goals were predominantly to see the overthrow of the Qing dynasty and its replacement with a democratic republic. The last Qing emperor abdicated in 1912 and China became a republic. This was not the last upheaval though. Having abolished the monarchy, after two thousand years of rule, the loose alliance of nationalists and communists who had led the uprisings and toppled the emperor began to fall apart. A new revolution emerged, this time a communist revolution to topple the nationalist government which had just been created.

The revolutions of the twentieth century would take China from; a feudal, agrarian society too weak to oppose the American and Europeans who sought to exploit the country; to a world superpower around which the world economy pivots.

10.1 - China at the end of the 19th century

The eventual defeat of the Taiping rebellion left China's economy devastated. Millions of lives had been lost and crops destroyed. The loss of income to the country was exacerbated by the cost of raising and equipping the armies needed to defeat the forces of the Heavenly Kingdom. The Qing dynasty was also facing aggressive foreign powers intent on the exploitation of China while lacking either the manpower or military technology to oppose them. This weakness in the face of the superior European forces of the French and British had been demonstrated in the two Opium Wars of the 1850's and the eventual razing of the Emperors Palace in Beijing in 1860.

The treaties China was forced to accept to end the foreign aggression gave foreign warships unlimited access to China's rivers, and therefore huge swathes of the interior. Foreigners were given special status which effectively meant they were above the law, answerable only to their own people and not the Chinese authorities. The second half of the nineteenth century saw China as a cash cow for the Western powers, with humiliation piled upon humiliation. The defeat of the Taiping was followed by further revolts such as the Miao Rebellion (1854 - 1873), the Panthay Rebellion (1856 - 1873) and the Dungan Revolt (1862 - 1877).

The Qing dynasty was intensely conservative in nature and therefore resistance to reform and modernization. Government posts were decided by examination which placed greater emphasis on a knowledge of literature, philosophy and the arts than any technical expertise and the common people had no outlet for their discontent. As a result, China found itself stagnating in a medieval, feudal system based around an agrarian economy which couldn't keep up with the Western powers or even its immediate neighbours; Japan and Russia. Conditions for the peasants were much as they had been for two thousand years. Discontent was repressed brutally, political opposition crushed.

However, even the conservative imperial court was forced, by the 1860's, to consider reform, simply to survive.

10.2 - The Hundred Days of Reform

The Hundred Days of Reform was a period of 104 days in which political, educational, social and economic reforms were attempted. It followed the ascendancy of a new emperor and final victory by Qing generals over the ethnic rebellions that had plagued the Han Chinese elite for most of the nineteenth century. The Tongzhi Emperor took the throne in 1861. He was five years old, leaving the government in the hands of his officials who began to pass through a number of modernising reforms. Zeng Goufan, who had led the Hunan army against the Taiping, was one of the chief architects of reform along with Li Hongzhang and Prince Gong. Together they began to adopt Western military technology and tactics. A foreign ministry was established and a modern army and navy.

The so-called Self Strengthening Movement was aimed at military and institutional reform rather than social or economic. It followed defeats for China at the hands of Britain in the First Opium War (1839 - 1842) and the Second Opium War (1856 - 1860). There had also been a humiliating defeat to the Japanese in the Sino-Japanese War of 1894-1895. This, in particular, was considered a deep shame as Japan had always been looked on as the inferior nation to China thus far. What the reformers noted was that while China had begun importing Western military technology and adopting Western military tactics, the westernisation of China had gone no further. Japan, meanwhile, had westernised both its military and its society, adopting a Parliamentary system of government. These changes appeared to have given lowly Japan the edge over their Chinese neighbours.

These Self Strengthening reforms did nothing to address the grievances of the peasants who had risen in such numbers to support the Taiping and other uprisings. Nor did it enable China to hold against successive incursions by foreign powers. Over the second half of the nineteenth-century Chinese territories were seized by France, Japan and Russia in a string of military defeats for China.

The Tongzhi Emperor died and was succeeded by the Guangzhou Emperor, who was more ambitious in his ideas for reform. He initiated a program of change which became known as the Hundred Days Reforms. These covered; changing the absolute monarchy to a constitutional monarchy, teaching maths and sciences in schools (not just Confucian philosophy), teaching Western liberal arts and sciences in university.

Those behind the Hundred Days Reforms believed that total social and institutional changes were needed, not just Self Strengthening. However, they were opposed by powerful court elements who were both anti-foreigner and conservative. The focus of court conservatives was the regent Empress Dowager Cixi. The reformist elements of the court had made a plan to have the Empress Dowager arrested and imprisoned.

However, they were betrayed by their agent who revealed the plot to the Empress' allies. In return, the Empress and her conservative allies staged a coup to remove the Guangzhou Emperor. The coup was staged in 1888, forcing Guangzhou into exile. Cixi took power as regent. The reforms which had been enacted were rescinded and six of the reforms' chief advocates were executed. These came to be known as the Six Gentlemen. Two more reform leaders, Kang Youwei and Liang Qichao fled China to Japan where they continued campaigning for a constitutional monarchy.

In 1906, the Qing government began establishing new schools and encouraged students to study abroad. This created a new social grouping of young intellectuals who were exposed to foreign ideas and would play a pivotal role in the coming revolution.

10.3 - The seeds of revolution

The reforms put forward between June 11th and September 22nd, 1898 may have been too radical a change for the inherently conservative Chinese, with too much being put forward and too quickly. Some of the reforms would be enacted a decade later which would seem to support this. The acceptance of some reform occurred after the Boxer Rebellion in Northern China in 1900. The Boxers were a group originating in northern China who marched on Beijing urging the Emperor to deport all Christians and foreigners from China. They were anti-foreigner, anti-Christian and anti-colonialist in their outlook and fearing that the increasing foreign involvement in Chinese affairs was leading it down the road of becoming a vassal state to Western powers. Foreigners in Beijing took refuge within the Legation Quarter where they were quickly besieged by the protesters. Empress Dowager Cixi declared her support for the Boxers and issued a declaration of war against the Western nations. The result of this was an eight national alliance including Britain, Russia and America, intent on bringing the rebellion under control and protecting their own interests within China.

The Eight-Nation Alliance landed in China with a force of 20,000 troops. They defeated the Imperial Chinese army and lifted the siege of the Legation Quarter of Beijing. When the peace treaty was signed, China was forced to accept a Western military presence in its capital as well as paying war reparations to the allies.

It was another humiliating defeat at the hands of vastly superior Western powers and it seems to have prompted the conservative Empress Dowager to begin to modernise China. Officials were dispatched to Japan and Europe to observe and draw up plans for reforms of Chinese government, law and social policy. One of the most significant of these reforms occurred soon after the end of the Boxer Rebellion when, in 1905, the system of imperial examinations was abolished. But the reforms that were enacted did not go far enough. For many, there was no alternative but to rebel. For those who had been campaigning for reform, the constant frustration of the conservative Qing court had led them to believe that only the complete overthrow of the monarchy would allow for the scope of reforms which they wished to see. These radicals would not be satisfied with the breadth of reform which Cixi was willing to see enacted and they would continue their campaign both in China and abroad.

In the 1890's and into the early twentieth century there was no shortage of Qing opponents living in exile in Japan or the United States. The Qing policy of suppression of political opponents, using arrest and execution as an everyday tool of statecraft, led to many radical intellectuals fleeing for their lives. From the relative safety of other countries, they continued to campaign and recruit support for a change in their home country.

These included the Furen Literary Society, found by Yeung Ku-wan and existing to satirise the Qing dynasty in print. Sun Yat-sen would emerge as the leader of one of the most influential anti-Qing movements. His Huaxinghui (Revive China Society) would merge with the Furen Literary

Society in 1894. Sun Yat-sen's main objective was to raise funds for revolution. In 1905 Sun Yat-sen merged the Huaxinghui with the Guanghui (Restoration Society) which was based in Shanghai. The new group would be instrumental in fermenting revolution in China and overthrowing the Qing dynasty. It was called the Tongmenghui (United League). Based principally in Tokyo its members were spread across a range of places and revolutionary groups. Members were predominantly in their late teens to their late twenties.

The revolts against the Qing government began in 1895, with the First Guangzhou uprising, organised by the Revive China Society, led by Sun Yat-sen It was put down by the government with its leaders arrested or fleeing into exile. But it was the first of many. There would be fifteen more between 1895 and 1911, all defeated. Then came the Wuchang Rising.

10.4 - The First Revolution

The first successful uprising of the revolution occurred in the Wuchang province. The Furen Literary Society and the Progressive Association were the principal groups involved, with the spark provided by protests over the Qing plan to nationalise railways built with local investment and sell them to foreign investors to reduce debts owed to overseas banks. In Sichuan Province many landowners and gentry and purchased shares in the Sichuan-Hankou Railway Company. Progress on construction had been slow and the government decided to take over, compensating shareholders with government bonds. On May 9th the nationalisation of all locally controlled railways was announced. Two days later a loan was agreed with the Four Powers Consortium which consisted of banks from Britain, America, France and Germany.

Shareholders in the Sichuan-Hankou venture were unhappy at being compensated in bonds for the silver they had paid for their shares. The

Railway Protection League was formed on June 17th, 1911 to organise protests at the privately owned property being seized by the Manchu court and sold to foreign powers. Between August 11th - 13th, more than ten thousand protesters gathered in the town Chengdu. Strikes and boycotts were organised and the leader of the Railway Protection League, Pu Dianjun, urged the Sichuan people to withhold taxes from the Qing government.

When Pu Dianjun was arrested, the protesters marched on the Chengdu police station to demand his release. Sichuan governor Zhao Erfeng ordered troops to fire on the protesters and thirty-two were killed. As the killings further inflamed the protester's anti-Qing groups such as the Tongmenghui further stoked the flames by inciting armed conflict against government troops. By mid-September, almost a thousand armed protesters were marching on Chengdu vowing to remove the governor.

In an attempt to quell the unrest, the Qing government removed Erfang from office and offered full compensation to all shareholders. But it was too late, as more than one hundred thousand insurgents were by then fighting against government authorities throughout the province. The Qing administration ordered soldiers from neighbouring Hubei and Hunan to be deployed in support of Sichuan troops. Protests in Hubei over the nationalisations had been smaller and therefore the risk of uprising deemed much lower. However, anti-Qing underground groups saw an opportunity as the province's soldiery were removed to quell the uprising in Sichuan.

On October the 10th, 1911, revolutionaries in the army launched an uprising in the town of Wuchang. The uprising was a success, the first successful uprising of the revolution. In a single morning, the revolutionaries had secured the town, declaring themselves the Military Government of Hubei of the Republic of China. The Wangchu uprising opened the floodgates to anti-Qing dynasty revolts across the country. Not all were motivated by the same goals but all would share the common theme of the overthrow of the Manchu rule and the desire to be part of the emerging Republic of China.

10.5 - Formation of the Republic

The Qing government fought back with their New Army (formed along Western lines and using Western arms during the Self Strengthening initiative) and retook many towns and cities that had rebelled. But the revolution could not be contained. By November 1911 almost two-thirds of China's 24 provinces had declared themselves independent of the Qing Empire. The imperial court recognised that negotiation was the only option left. Yuan Shikai was appointed as Prime Minister on November 1st, 1911. On November 3rd the government passed the Nineteenth Articles which amended the role of the Qing dynasty from absolute monarchs to that of a constitutional monarchy. By December, the revolutionaries had set up a provisional government in Nanking, while the Qing dynasty governed from Beijing. Despite the revolutionary gains the country was now polarised between north and south, with the southern provinces in revolutionary hands and the north still in Qing control.

A conference was held on December 18th to discuss the issues. Tang Shaoyi was chosen as the representative of the Qing dynasty and Wu Tingfang for the revolutionaries. A British businessman, Edward Selby Little, acted as mediator in the peace negotiations that followed. An agreement was reached that allowed the revolutionary-held southern provinces to support a republican government headed by Yuan Shikai, provided the emperor abdicate his throne. The Manchu dynasty was ended after more than three hundred years of power. The reign of the Chinese emperors was over after more than two thousand years.

Sun Yat-sen was elected the first provisional president of the Republic of China on December 29th, 1911. He was inaugurated in the revolutionary capital he had established in Nanjing. Prime Minister Yuan Shikai had control over the former imperial forces of the New Army and led a rival Republican government in Beijing. Seeking to avoid civil war, with its concomitant risk of foreign invasion, Sun Yat-sen agreed to accept Shikai's Beijing government as the single government of the Republic.

10.6 - The Second Revolution

On March 10th 1912, Shikai was inaugurated as the second provisional president of the Republic of China. His power, based on the control of the Republic's only army, soon began to eclipse that of the fledgeling Parliament, verging on the dictatorial. It seemed that one absolute monarch may have been overthrown in favour of another. In August the Kuomintang (KMT) was founded by Song Jiaoren. It brought together several smaller political groups including Sun Yat-sen's Tongmenghui. By amalgamating the smaller nationalist parties the hope was to form a power bloc that would be able to neutralise the power of the president. In 1913 elections the KMT secured a majority of seats.

Song was assassinated in March 1913, just a month after his party secured a majority in Parliament. Shikai's involvement was not proven but it was known he had used assassination as a tool to eliminate other political rivals. In April he secured a loan from a group of foreign powers without consultation with parliament and used it to finance the army. Resentment was growing against him. The Kuomintang accused him of abusing his position, while they, in turn, were accused of inciting civil war.

In July, seven of twenty-four provinces had risen in rebellion. This second revolution was partly driven by the dictatorial tendencies of the President and a resentment among veterans of the first revolution that power now rested in the hands of former Qing dynasty officials, instead of men like Sun Yat-sen who had fought. The rebellion was crushed and Sun Yat-sen and the other revolutionary leaders fled into exile once again.

10.7 - The Chinese Communist Party

By November the Kuomintang was ordered dissolved Shikai. As they formed the majority party in parliament, without them the body lost its legitimacy and became an irrelevance. In February 1914 Shikai ordered an amendment to the constitution which granted him greater powers such as the right to sign treaties without the consent of parliament or to declare war. He extended the term over which the president served for ten years. Increasingly, Yuan Shikai was making himself into an emperor.

In July 1914, Sun Yat-sen was trying to rebuild his Republican party, from the remnants of the KMT and the defeat of the second revolution. He began building a coalition, including former opponents such as the Progressive Party, which had sided with Shikai during the Second Revolution. Shikai's allies were gradually deserting him, provincial governors who had declared their provinces independent of the Qing dynasty were wary of his increasingly monarchical rule, the Progressive Party disliked his sidelining of parliament.

In 1915, Yuan Shikai declared himself emperor of the Chinese Empire and sealed the fate of the Beijing government as the single government of a united China. By 1917, Shikai was dead, his son had briefly succeeded him and then relinquished the position as China degenerated into warlordism. New Army generals and provincial governors in command of troops carved out kingdoms of their own. Meanwhile, both Russia and Japan were claiming slices of Chinese territory previously claimed by the Germans.

The southern provinces declared their independence in 1916, led by Yunnan province on December 25th, 1915. In Guangzhou province, Sun Yat-sen established a government to rival that of Beijing, where former general Duan Qirui was following in the footsteps of Shikai in making himself a dictator in disregard of the constitution. He established a Constitutional Protection Army with which to counter the national army which the president had under his control.

In October 1919, he reformed the KMT and spent the next two years as president of the southern government, trying to recruit support from various western nations. None was willing to support the revolutionaries against the internationally recognised Beijing government except the Soviet Union. They provided support for both Sun Yat-sen and the fledgeling Chinese Communist Party. The emergence of the Communist party was to be pivotal over the next twenty years. As the Soviets increased their commitment to helping reunify China, sending advisors to help Sun Yat-sen's government, they also encouraged the Chinese Communist Party (CCP) to move into the KMT power bloc. For all parties, this was a matter of expediency. Both Soviets and CCP had an interest in ensuring that Communists played a role in the unification of China and the re-establishment of the Republic. The Chinese Communists were still in their infancy as a political party and could affect change on their own.

The KMT had seen their alliance with warlord factions dissolve and they needed to build strong alliances, accepting the Communists was a necessary step to acquiring the support they needed. The Soviets helped to create the First United Front. One of Sun's lieutenants, Chiang Kai-shek was selected for training in Moscow and on his return helped establish a military academy at Whampoa, just outside the southern seat of government.

Sun Yat-sen died in March 1925 and Chiang Kai-Shek succeeded him as commander-in-chief of the National Revolutionary Army. He embarked on a campaign against the northern warlords and within a year had conquered half of China. The nationalist movement was once again gaining momentum but the United Front was becoming increasingly polarised between left and right. Within the Front, the CCP had been growing in numbers steadily increasing the influence of the left wing of the party. Kai-Shek began to take steps in 1926 to restrict the power of the left, preventing them from taking positions in the leadership and increasing his own power as a result.

Finally, in 1927 the party split entirely. The Communists established their own capital at Wuhan, Kai-Shek established an anti-communist government in Nanjing and the old government was still based in Beijing. Ultimately, Kai-Shek's anti-communist, the nationalist government would gain the upper hand bringing all of China under his control and achieving international recognition as the official capital of the Republic of China.

The CCP had been ousted by the KMT left wingers from Wuhan and had attempted to raise numerous rebellions, all of which were crushed by Kai-Shek's nationalists. He embarked on an anti-communist crusade to wipe out the CCP and this produced an event which would cement the reputation of one Mao Zedong among his Communist comrades, and seal the fate of the nationalists. Zedong had been part of a Communist force surrounded by the Nationalists. They had embarked on a nine thousand kilometre march to the north in order to escape from their stronghold in Jiangxi province. What became known as the Long March took over a year to complete and only a tenth of the Communists survived. However, it was the beginning of the rise to power of Zedong.

10.8 - The Communist Revolution

Zedong's Long March occurred in 1934. By 1939 as Germany triggered the beginning of World War Two, China was facing incursions into Manchuria by the Japanese. When Japan allied itself with Germany, this brought China into alignment with the Allies. Under the Nationalist government of Chiang Kai-Shek had begun to modernise and reform China's economy and society up to this point.

But the war against Japan, as well as a series of costly wars that ravaged western China drained Kai-Shek's government resources. Increasingly their control was over the eastern provinces as the Communists gathered strength in the north. It was the north where the Soviets had ousted the Japanese during the war and given Japanese machinery and equipment to the People's Liberation Army. The situation was exacerbated by rampant government corruption and profiteering. Following the war, there was widespread starvation and the country stood on the brink of civil war. A century earlier, the Taipings had given the poorest of China the opportunity to better themselves, had offered support to those parts of Chinese society worst hit by famine and drought. Now the CCP did the same and succeeded in building a Communist network among the rural communities of China. The Nationalists in power in Nanjing received loans from the United States while the ordinary people suffered. They devoted their energy to stamping out the communists while the CCP took the side of the peasants in land and tax reforms.

Both Nationalists and Communists worked together during the war against the Japanese but once the war was over the alliance dissolved. The United States refused to support Nanjing with troops, though their provided financial aid. From 1945 to 1949 the KMT forces fought a losing battle against a highly motivated and disciplined People's Liberation Army. Beijing was surrendered without a shot in January 1949. Other major cities followed suit. On October 1st, Kai-Shek fled China for Taiwan along with approximately two million refugees and a hundred thousand Nationalist troops.

On September 21st, 1949, Communist Party Chairman, Mao Zedong declared the establishment of the People's Republic of China. The civil war between nationalists and communists had raged for twenty years from 1927 to 1949. It had claimed an estimated 3.5 million lives including non-combatants. More lives were to be claimed by the successive revolutions inflicted on mainland China by the ruling Communist party under Mao.

As part of land reforms designed to find favour with the peasant class, approximately one million landowners were executed. Then came the Great Leap Forward, between 1958 and 1961 during which the party attempted to convert China's agrarian economy to an industrial one in a short space of time. This resulted in famine, as agricultural land was forcibly converted to industrial use, reducing food production at the same time as the population had almost doubled. The Great Chinese Famine cost an estimated forty-five million lives.

Further upheaval was to follow as Mao sought to reinforce his own ideology and that of the Communist party. This would come to be known as the Cultural Revolution. It began in 1966 and was declared to be over by Mao in 1969 (though its practices continued until after Mao's death in 1976. It was a purge throughout the Party and China itself of all those who were deemed to be enemies of the revolution (capitalists and those who still followed Chinese traditions). It led to a purge of senior party officials and the formation of Red Guards across China. These were groups of youths who appeared across the country and carried out Mao's wish to see anything that did not to conform to Maoist Communism stamped out.

To this end, there were violent struggles across all walks of life and throughout China. Millions were persecuted, tortured or suffered the loss of property, imprisonment or even execution. The Down to the Countryside Movement saw the forcible displacement of a large portion of the population as youths were moved from urban to rural areas. Any artefact of history or religion was destroyed.

10.9 - Aftermath

In half a century China had been transformed from a feudal, agrarian society to an industrial and economic powerhouse at the leading edge of the modern world. It had been ruled by a monarchy that had become fossilised over two thousand years of rigid adherence to tradition, a monarchy that was incapable of the kind of rapid change increasingly demanded by its people. That would be swept aside in the most violent and brutal way imaginable, resulting in a loss of life incomprehensible to a modern Westerner, as the Chinese state was literally torn apart and rebuilt from the ground up.

The Chinese people had experienced a taste of democracy and personal freedom in the 1850's under the progressive influence of the Heavenly Kingdom. Despite the Kingdom's demise and the brutal repression of political opponents, the genie refused to be put back into the bottle. From the 1850's onwards China was wracked by revolts and uprisings led by the underclasses of Chinese society. A tradition began of seeking revolution to overturn a corrupt, elitist, hated regime.

First, this regime was the ethnic minority Manchu government of the Qing Empire. Unwilling and unable to provide social and land reforms, or to free China from its vassal status to numerous Western powers, the Qing emperors left no option for reform other than revolution. Even when the Qing dynasty was ended, the monarchy abolished, China found itself drifting back into a dictatorship which in turn led to an extended and destructive civil war between north and south, followed by another civil war between nationalists and communists.

It was only at the conclusion of this second civil war, with the ascension of the Communist party and the creation of the People's Republic of China that the revolutionary ideals of the 1850's were finally achieved. The cost in blood for these reforms was significant, with the death toll from the Great Leap Forward alone probably equalling that of the half-century of armed conflict which had gone to make it possible.

There is a connecting line which can be drawn through the Taiping Rebellion in the mid-eighteenth century and the desire for social and economic reform to the battle between Communists and corrupt Nationalists one hundred years later. The Taipings fought for the poorest people and against a corrupt, elitist regime supported by foreign powers and which appeared to care little for reforms that would help the common people at the expense of its own power. That regime was the Qing Empire. By the 1950's the Communists were fighting for the people against a regime that was rife with corruption and being propped up by the United States in order to prevent China becoming a Communist state.

The struggle of Sun Yat-sen against the last of the Qing dynasty and then against the dictatorial Yuan Shikai was the same. Though possessed of differences and separated by time, these events can be viewed as a continuous struggle for a people to emerge from the darkness of a feudal society into the modern world. The cost in blood of this century of revolution is enormous and there are few revolutions in history that can match it.

CHAPTER 11

THE SPANISH CIVIL WAR

Introduction

The Spanish Civil War was a conflict fought between 1936 to 1939 between a democratic, left-leaning revolutionary force and a counter-revolutionary, right-wing movement. The war began with an attempt to overthrow the democratic Second Spanish Republic, formed in 1931 by a group of generals. The uprising split the country between those who supported the communist and socialist parties of the Republic and the right wing Nationalists. The Republicans (a loose alliance of anarchists, republicans, communists and socialists) were supported by the Soviet Union and Mexico, while individuals from many other states joined the International Brigades in order to fight against the rise of fascism. The Nationalist forces were commanded by Francisco Franco and backed by the Nazi government of Germany and the Italian regime of Mussolini.

The conflict became perceived as a fight between democracy and fascism and this fact made it an attractive cause to individuals from Britain, France and America amongst other countries. The Nationalist forces overpowered the Republicans and by 1939 Franco had declared himself the victor. His government was subsequently recognised by the international community. Once securely in power Franco became a dictator who would rule over Spain until 1975. Thousands of Republicans fled to refugee camps in Southern France. Franco's regime persecuted those who had opposed it. The Spanish Civil War was notable for the intervention of Nazi Germany who took the opportunity to test the efficacy of the Luftwaffe as an air superiority force. The most infamous example of this was the bombing of the town of Guernica.

The war was also about more than just a clash of democracy versus fascism, though in the popular imagination this is what has been most clearly remembered. On the Nationalist side were conservatives from rural backgrounds as well as monarchists and Catholics. So it was a conflict between the urban and the rural, secular and religious, traditionalist and radical. The Spanish Civil War was in many ways, the conclusion of more than a century of upheaval, coups and struggles for power between reformers and conservatives. To understand the causes of the Spanish Civil War it is first necessary to examine the situation the country found itself in through the nineteenth century.

11.1 - Nineteenth century Spain

Spain found itself under the rule of the French in the first decade of the nineteenth century, with Napoleon Bonaparte installing his brother Joseph on the Spanish throne. The Spanish and British fought to free Spain, and by 1812 had succeeded. This was the beginning of a liberal movement in Spain, seeking universal suffrage and land reform in the absence of a ruling monarch. The long fight to liberate Spain led to the existence of an extensive officer class and a large number of highly experienced guerilla fighters. These factions were, for the most part, liberal in their outlook, influenced by the Enlightenment and the principles of the French Revolution.

They were opposed by ultra-conservatives who believed in an autocratic monarchy.

In the first half of the nineteenth century, Spain was an agricultural economy. The land was held by a small elite who also dominated government positions. This rural economy was threatened by the gradual loss of Spanish overseas territories in North America, Mexico, Central and South America resulting in a bankrupting of the Spanish state. This led to a great deal of social unrest and the further polarisation of political factions into liberals and conservatives.

By 1868, the Bourbon monarchy of Queen Isabella II was overthrown in a series of popular revolts, inspired by poverty and a resentment of the ultra-conservative nature of the Spanish monarchy. In the absence of a monarch, the First Spanish Republic was formed though it only lasted for just over a year before the Bourbon dynasty was restored to the throne.

The nineteenth century for Spain was characterised by a series of wars; the Carlist civil wars occurred mid-century as an attempt to overthrow one monarch in favour of another branch of the family, believed to have a more legitimate claim. Under Queen Isabella II a series of fruitless foreign wars were also fought. By the end of the century, a disastrous war against the United States led to the liberation of Spain's last imperial possessions in the Caribbean and the Pacific, such as Cuba, Puerto Rico and the Philippines. At this point, the large officer class found itself redundant. They had been formed as part of the Spanish military machine to protect its overseas territories and to liberate Spain from the French. Now, the military function of this officer elite was removed. It began a movement to a more political role which would be of significance to the events of the twentieth century.

11.2 - Twentieth-century Spain

Among the military officers there emerged a belief that Spain's humiliating defeats were the fault of incompetent and corrupt civilian politicians. The French occupation and subsequent guerrilla war had left a tradition of rebellion as a legitimate means of change. By the time a young Francisco Franco entered a military academy in 1907, there was an entrenched view that the defence of Spain's traditions, institutions and the restoration of its former glory was the responsibility of the military. A generation was growing up that saw itself as the opponents of the forces of change and liberalism.

By the 1920's new urban centres were emerging and fledgeling industries. With these new industries came a new social class. They were urban and consisted of both professional and industrial classes. In contrast to this was traditional Spain, characterised by regions of Central Spain. These areas remained rural and predominantly consisted of small villages and market towns. In these areas, agriculture was the heart of the economy and the Catholic Church was the glue which held these communities together. These were bastions of tradition and conservatism.

The role of the Church in Spanish society was also in decline, except for these central regions. In the new urban areas, the Catholic church had little influence over the new professional classes or the urban workers. In southern Spain, agriculture consisted of large-scale plantations on which workers with no rights to the land they worked, were virtual slaves. In the south, the Church was seen as the supporter of the hated landed gentry and their various tools of oppression and thus was rejected by the peasant class.

Spain remained neutral during the First World War, but the example of the Russian Revolution led to a deep suspicion of civil protest by the ruling elite. In Barcelona, a powerful trade union committed to violent actions against employers who would not acknowledge workers' rights. The fight to reduce the influence of this union led to a coup in 1923 by General Miguel Primo de Rivera and a military dictatorship. The formation of political parties was illegal in 1920's Spain but the new professional classes began to form professional associations in order to protect their own interests against the arbitrary rule of a military dictator.

The rule of Primo de Rivera was brought to an end in January 1930 by his attempts to bring about reform of the army and labour rights. He was opposed in this by the army and the vested interests of the landed elites. Following the deposing of Primo de Rivera the king, Ferdinand VII, found himself under increasing pressure from all sides, supported only by the Church. On the 14th April 1931, the King abdicated and the Second Spanish Republic was formed. The First Spanish Republic had lasted for a year in the mid-nineteenth century after the overthrow of the Bourbon dynasty.

11.3 - The Second Spanish Republic

The Republican administration was a reforming government. It comprised an alliance between a professional, clerical class of lawyers and teachers along with the socialists. Together these two groups sought social reform (such as a welfare state) and structural reform to modernise the Spanish economy and open it up to the rest of Europe. They sought to enfranchise the landless peasants of the south, giving them land and the means to better themselves. The church was to be separated from the state and removed entirely from the education system. The army was to brought under civilian control with the officer class reduced in number, freeing up funds for further economic reforms.

The proposed reforms of the Republicans and the Socialists targeted traditional vested interest; Church, landowners and the army. Several bishops spoke out against the move to a secular state, with one forced into exile for his outspoken attack on the Republic. There was also unrest among the traditional, conservative villagers and towns of central Spain. Here, the Church was still an important part of personal and community life. The reforms being proposed by the Republicans threatened the practice of religious ceremonies and the observance of rituals. While the Republicans were attempting to reform the institutions of Spain, a structural reform, they were impinging on personal matters of belief and piety. This produced a great deal of resentment.

The officer class had begun an isolated group, centred around the military academies. Not only did they see the military as the guardians of Spain's former greatness but they did not mix with other social groups, further cementing their reactionary views. These views were deepened by the attempt to establish a new overseas colony in Morocco. The officers of this overseas force came to be known as the Africanistas and they became a hotbed for conservative nationalism. Franco, himself, was one of these.

In 1927 Franco became the commandant of a military academy at Zaragoza. The chain of command he established there was dominated by Africanistas and the academy became a breeding ground for ideas of imperialism, the corruption and weakness of the urban classes and the Republic itself. In the Zaragoza academy, Franco could not only build an ultra-loyal cadre of experienced military leaders but he could influence an entire generation to his nationalist agenda. In September 1931 the Republican administration sought to close the Zaragoza academy. In so doing they were attacking the livelihoods of those who had chosen the military path, removing a means of advancement while also attempting to reduce the number of officers in the army entirely.

The attempt to curtail the expenses of the army, by reducing numbers of officers, and close the Zaragoza academy led to two coups. One in 1932 was unsuccessful, the second in 1936 was different.

In 1936 an alliance had formed on the right wing of Spanish politics. Siding with the army and the Church were the lay people who saw themselves as defenders of a dying way of life. There were also the Carlists, ultra-conservative monarchists who organised themselves along military lines to achieve their goals. By attempting to separate Church and state and reduce the power and influence of Catholic priests by barring them from education, the Republicans had mobilised the right-leaning elements of Spanish society in a rabid, hatred of Republicanism, liberalism and democracy.

11.4 - Downfall of the Second Republic

The Republic had an immediate problem in that while it could enact legislation in Parliament. The reforms contained in that legislation had little or no chance of being enforced when faced with the intransigent vested interests of the traditional elites. Land and social reform in the south were ignored by the landowners and the police who remained in their traditional role as enforcers of the orders of the landowners. Brutal repression of peasants continued despite the Republic's best intentions. This served to begin to alienate those peasants, who had seen the rise of the Republic as their saviour. Those same peasants now began to become disillusioned. The promised social reform of the Republicans increasingly looking like unachievable dreams.

The Republican reforms were aimed at generating wealth which in turn would fund further modernisation and structural improvements. So, when the landless, dispossessed and increasingly disillusioned poor protested against their lot they were often met by Republican security forces. There were clashes resulting in deaths in Castilblanco in December 1931, Arnedo and Barcelona in January 1932 and in Andalucia in January 1933. These sudden explosions of violence were the highlights of a grim, daily situation. Amongst those the Republican police found themselves fighting were those who were refusing to pay rent and street traders catering to the poorest in society. Both groups were attacked at the behest of wealthier social groups more inclined to support the conservatives (such as landlords and shopkeepers) but to maintain law and order the Republican administration found themselves alienating their natural supporters.

A conservative government was elected in 1933 following the collapse of the Left-wing alliance of socialists, communists and anarchists who had formed the Republican government. In 1934 there was widespread disorder as Spain was gripped by economic depression and the new government sought to overturn any reforms already enacted by their predecessors. In particular young people on both sides of the political divide were becoming increasingly radicalised and mobilised.

In October 1934 a general strike was attempted. It failed to take root in most areas but in the coal mining, northern regions of the Asturias there was an armed rebellion. General Franco, as head of the War Ministry, led the repression of these rebels. The air force was used to bomb the rebels, the navy to shell coastal towns and villages. Distrusting native forces, Franco made use of Moroccan and Foreign Legion troops on the ground to overrun the rebels. After their defeat there followed a period of brutal repression.

Unions were abolished and their premises closed. So too were the premises of political parties opposed to the government. Around thirty thousand people with left-leaning political sympathies were rounded up, tortured and in some cases executed. It was in this atmosphere of violence and repression that those on the Left in Spain realised that they could never prevail in a violent act of force against the Right. The Right-wing was the legitimate government and could call upon all the apparatus of the state to overcome their adversaries. Instead, the loose coalition of Leftist parties would need to show greater cohesion and political unity. The only way to win was at the ballot box.

A progressive, liberal alliance won the next election, in February 1936. Their platform was to re-enact the social and structural reforms of the first Republican government. To prevent this government from achieving its goals the military staged a coup, on the 17th of July 1836. It began in the Spanish North African colony of Morocco and quickly spread to mainland Spain through a series of garrison revolts. It was the intention of the rebels to seize control of the country, which they failed to do. However, they seized enough that the government's reform agenda was effectively stalled. The rebels held northern and western Spain while the Republicans held southern and eastern Spain.

11.5 - Outbreak of Civil War

Following the attempted coup, Spain was divided. Even the army, which had been a bastion of conservatism and anti-Republicanism thanks to its officer corps, was split. The Navy joined the Republicans, preventing rebel forces such as the Army of Africa and the Foreign Legion from being mobilised on the mainland. There were instances of rebel forces executing their own officers when those officers revealed Republican sympathies. It was the fractured nature of the Spanish armed forces that led the leaders of the rebellion to request aid from their political cousins overseas; namely the other Fascist states of Europe, Germany and Italy.

Both contributed aircraft to airlift elite overseas based troops into mainland Spain. The German air force also used the civil war to test it's fledgeling bomber capabilities. This was not the only violence inflicted on those who found themselves living in the Republican-held territory. The split of the nation, army and police had effectively paralysed the government, whose control and authority broke down outside the urban centres. Everywhere else local people found themselves able to make their own law. This seems to have produced an outbreak of violent action targeting those who had opposed the reforms of the previous Republican administrations. This included some seven thousand priests and other

Catholic church officials, in revenge killings for the role which the Church had historically played in blocking reform and modernisation.

Mass murders were also occurring in rebel-held territory, again as a result of localist power with little or no strong, central authority. Amid propaganda from all sides of the rebel political alliance came the message that Spain needed to remain whole, that Spain needed to be strong and that to achieve this a purge was needed. As locals in the Republican-held territory had taken the opportunity to avenge political wrongs so too did rebels in the areas of the country which they controlled. In Republican areas, the killings were to produce a new world, to allow the birth of a Spain that had not existed before. In rebel areas, the killings were to maintain the old world, but with the corrupting influences purged.

In July 1936, the Army of Africa landed in southern Spain. It comprised soldiers of the Foreign Legion and Moroccan mercenaries commanded by Spanish officers (the Africanistas - of which Franco had been one). Franco was in overall command of the force. They swept through southern Spain unopposed and enacted a brutal punishment on Republican supporters and the rural peasantry of the south. In many cases, the owners of plantations had relatives who were officers in the army and they followed Franco's advance in order to reclaim their lands which had been divided up between the previously landless peasantry by Republican reformers.

There was a systemic campaign of terror enacted across the villages of the south; including torture, rape and murder. Franco represented the views of the Army of Africa's officers. He stated publicly that all resistance in Republican-held areas should be annihilated. When interviewed by an American journalist he stated his objective was to save Spain from Marxism 'whatever the cost', later in the same interview he acknowledged that killing half the population in order to save it fitted that definition of 'whatever the cost'. Franco treated the campaign not as a civil war against fellow

Spaniards but as a colonial war of repression. Those whose deaths he ordered were viewed in some way as foreigners, aliens who sought to subvert his Spain. As such there was no mercy given, Spain had to be purged of Republicanism. This view was reinforced by the Catholic Church, or at least by its Spanish branch. The Church supported the rebels and described them as crusaders. There are few conflicts in world history as bloody or as brutal as religious crusades.

11.6 - The Rise of Franco

In 1936, General Francisco Franco was just one general among the rebel forces. He held a prominent position but was not yet a dictator. The proclaimed leader of the rebellion was General Emilio Mola, but his campaign in the north had stalled. Franco, meanwhile, with his professional and experienced army supported with technical assistance from Germany and Italy, was advancing rapidly in the south. Franco employed terror as one of the principal weapons in his arsenal. Most of the opponents of his Army of Africa were civilians armed with whatever they could lay hands on. When the Army of Africa captured a Republican town or village the reprisals were brutal. Bodies were left in the streets for days and then burned without burial rites. Such was the brutality of the Army of Africa that it's fearsome reputation preceded it, and often Republicans fled before it, rather than fight or risk capture.

By the end of October 1936, Franco's forces were on the outskirts of Madrid. Along the way, he had gained a publicity coup with the capture of the city of Toledo, in which he had been filmed touring the aftermath of the battle. Following his 'liberation' of Toledo, a city with a great deal of significance for the Right because it had been the first Muslim held city to be liberated by the Christians in the middle ages, Franco found himself in the position of supreme commander of all rebel forces in the south, earning the title which he would hold for decades to come, 'generalissimo'.

But Franco's decision to divert to Toledo, while a political coup, was a tactical blunder. It gave time for the Soviet Union to send military aid to the Republicans. Until this point they had stood back from the conflict, seeking a close alliance with Britain and France against expansionist Germany. Britain was staunchly opposed to the Republic and the Soviet Union didn't want to risk British ire. But thanks to Franco's whirlwind advance it seemed German involvement in Spain would soon cease, freeing up the Luftwaffe to be moved to a potential attack upon the Soviet Union. To prolong the Spanish conflict, the Soviets sent tanks, planes and pilots to defend Madrid. The battle raged through the winter of 1936 and a stunning victory was achieved by the Republicans. Madrid became a symbol of the Republican struggle against fascism oppression.

Victories in Madrid and the surrounding area brought a great deal of public attention to the way. Writers and artists from across the world became interested in championing the Republican cause, describing it as the fight for a free culture against the tyranny of fascism. Those who wanted to play a more direct role also came. The International Brigades were units of volunteers from across the world, though predominantly European. At their peak, the International Brigades comprised some 35,000 volunteers. They came from many different countries, including those where right-wing nationalist regimes had arisen following the First World War. They comprised racial groups who had experienced persecution, such as the Jews and a small number of African-Americans (the Abraham Lincoln Brigade was the first non-segregated military unit in history). Regardless of race or nationality, all believed that the Spanish Civil War was the ultimate battle against the forces of fascism that seemed poised to sweep Europe.

With Franco's advance temporarily halted at Madrid, Mussolini decided to wholly commit his own country to the war. Some 75,000 Italian troops would enter the conflict, while the German restricted themselves to providing airpower and technological support. The use of airpower in the conflict was the first ever air raids take place against the population of Madrid. The Germans, in particular, used the Spanish conflict as an opportunity to train their bomber pilots for later conflicts. The civilian population of southern Spain had already been targeted by the rebels, now the urban population of Madrid came under attack. It was what is now known as 'total war'. The concept was little known then but is a terrible innovation of warfare that would come to be commonplace in world conflicts.

By this time the rebels were very much Franco's army, despite his official position being one of first among equals amongst the other rebel generals. It was Franco who most impressed Hitler and Mussolini, and was instrumental in obtaining their support. He was an opportunist who took the fullest advantage of the opportunities that came his way. Upon landing the Army of Africa in Spain, Franco had set up his own press office, already clearly planning to legitimise the rebellion by opening channels of communication to the Spanish people and the wider world. It was this press office that allowed Franco to maximise the publicity among his own supporters that came from the liberation of the Toledo garrison. Franco also lacked any firm political allegiance within the group that made up the rebel right-wingers. He was neither wholly monarchist or fascist but could appeal to all elements of the right wing.

While he was politically diverse enough to hold together the right-wingers in the rebellion he was also unshakeable and unerring in his own beliefs that he was fighting a crusade to save Spain. More than one of his fellow Africanistas commented that Franco was such a man who, if he captured the whole of Spain would never relinquish it. Upon being appointed supreme political and military commander of the rebel forces, they believed, Franco would take this to mean all that the rebels captured belonged to him, personally.

These opinions would turn out to be true. Franco would not relinquish his control until his death almost thirty years after the war. The brutality of the rebels was proof of his self-belief in the rightness of his cause. To Franco, the ends very much justified the means. To this end, terror was deployed as a military tactic, often against civilians. Air raids were used for the first time in Europe, most infamously at Guernica in the Basque territory, where a town was annihilated simply to ensure that the Basques had no further appetite to resist. There were certainly no military targets at Guernica and no air defences.

After initial rapid gains of territory, Franco adopted a strategy of attrition. He believed that a fast conquest, which would surely have been achievable given the German and Italian support he had, would not serve his purpose; to cleanse Spain of the Republican moral pollution. To do that he needed to control the people. Franco wanted the war to be as drawn out and difficult as possible, even at the expense of his own troops. And when the Republicans were finally defeated he wanted a new Spain to rise from the ashes. To Franco, the soldier was the perfect vessel to bring about the salvation of Spain, and a military hierarchy was the perfect structure for the new Spain. The military should have a position of pre-eminence over the civilian.

11.7 - The end of the Republic

When the Army of Africa had landed in Spain in 1936 the rebels would secure northwestern and western Spain but their territory was surrounded by Republican-held regions. The rebels were denied access to the north coast or the south coast other than the southwestern tip of Spain. By 1937 the entirety of northern and western Spain was in rebel hands, with the Republicans fighting desperately to hold Madrid and their access to the Mediterranean. Between 1938 and 1939, successful offensives by Franco led to the shrinking of Republican-held territory. With Mediterranean ports denied to them, the Republicans found it increasingly difficult to obtain supplies from the Soviet Union. France, initially non-interventionist in order to maintain its alliance with Britain and out of fear of the two militaristic, fascist nations on its borders (Germany and Italy) adopted a more flexible approach and allowed supplies to the Republicans across the land border between the two countries. By 1939 this two was cut off as Franco completed successful campaigns in Catalonia in the first two months of the year.

On March 5th, 1939, the Republican Army under the command of Colonel Sigismundo Casado, rose against the Republican government. Prime Minister Juan Negrin was overthrown and fled to France. A brief rebellion by communist forces in Madrid was suppressed and peace terms were offered to Franco. They were refused. Such was Franco's binary view, there could be only unconditional surrender and total victory. An offensive was launched on the 26th March and by the 31st the war was over.

11.8 - Aftermath

It will come as no surprise that Franco was equally as brutal in victory as he had been in war. Following the final surrender of the Republicans, there were reprisals against those deemed to be enemies of Spain. Estimates range from 30,000 to as many as 200,000 people were executed. Many more were forced into labour camps. Almost half a million refugees fled to France. There they only escaped fascism for a few short years before finding themselves under the control of the Vichy regime, as France fell to the Nazis. Spanish refugees were held in internment camps in France before many were repatriated back to Spain where they were imprisoned again, in a concentration camp at Miranda de Ebro. Around 5,000 Spanish refugees ended up being deported to Germany and subsequently dying in the Mauthausen concentration camp.

The repression of any who had sympathised with the Republicans or belonged to a Republican party was legalized by a law passed before the end of the war. The Law of Political Responsibilities was issued by Franco on February 13th, 1939. It declared membership of the Popular Front illegal. The Popular Front was a political party formed of a group of left-leaning parties to contest the 1936 election and ensure defeat for the right-wing nationalists. The Law imposed harsh penalties for past party membership and even imposed those penalties on the families of those found guilty, where the guilty party was deceased. It was also used as a justification for the continued 'purification' of Spain, the mantra under which many atrocities against those suspected of being Republican sympathizers was carried out.

The repression which took place after the war was an extension of the terror which had taken place as part of the military strategy. It became known as the 'white terror'. But this was not the only violence perpetrated against civilians during the War. Though on a different scale compared to the actions of the Fascists, violence also occurred in the Republican-held territory during the early years of the war. This was blamed on a breakdown of law and order, as the fledgeling Republican government could not effectively govern outside of Madrid. Known as the 'red terror' it saw some 38,000 extra-judicial killings. These were revenge killings, against supporters of the rebels or opponents of Republican reforms. They were also outlets of violence by those elements of Spanish society long denied a voice and finally able to strike back at the people who had oppressed them for so long.

The Spanish Civil War proved unsuccessful as a revolutionary movement. It was prompted by a fledgeling revolution against the conservative establishment. Had the Republican movement succeeded then the Spanish Civil War would probably be an example of a liberal, democratizing revolution and comparable to the French Revolution. But the inability of the Republicans to overcome intensely hostile vested interests, and the disparate nature of the Republican coalition, in comparison to the rabid unity of the military, doomed it to failure.

Republicans could not match the military might of the fascist movement, complete with support from two wealthy, highly militarised fascist states. It was also the case that the resolution of the fascists, to cleanse Spain, meant that they were unlikely ever to accept compromise. Franco and others like him approached the war as a religious crusade to restore Spain to a mythical golden age. The Republicans could not achieve total victory, they had neither the resources, the unity or the foreign support. They could not achieve it and no other outcome would save their revolution. Having failed to win they were utterly extinguished and Spain was returned to a state of dictatorship just as conservative and repressive as the worst of the monarchies.

CHAPTER 12

THE YOUNG TURKS

Introduction

The revolution known as the 'Young Turks' revolution occurred in 1908 in the Ottoman Empire. It was an attempt to restore a parliamentary democracy that been established and subsequently abolished, thirty years before. The ruler of the Empire, Sultan Abdul Hamid II allowed for the creation of a Parliament and then subsequently abolished it two years later. It was Abdul Hamid II who then restored the 1876 constitution in 1908.

The Sultans governed absolutely, with political power resting ultimately with him and a small coterie of advisors who were regularly changed. But there was an appetite for change and modernisation with the country from two particular social groups. One was liberal in their outlook and desired a 'hands off' government that would allow the economy to flourish and give them the freedom to make that happen. The other was the Unionists, working classes who desired a secular government.

The trigger point occurred when a group of military officers rebelled, believing that the policies of the Sultan were leading to the weakening of the state which they were sworn to defend. Initially successful, the revolt led to the restoration of the Ottoman Parliament and the institution of a secular government. However, this success was short lived. A series of wars led to provinces of the Ottoman Empire becoming independent. The Empire sought an alliance with Germany and this led to the disintegration of the Empire following the First World War.

12.1 - Background

The Ottoman Empire had its origins in the region of Anatolia, which is now part of modern-day Turkey. In the fourteenth and fifteenth centuries, the Empire expanded into eastern Europe with the conquest of the Balkans and then Constantinople, an event which brought about the downfall of the Byzantine Empire. Between the fourteenth and seventeenth centuries, the Empire expanded to cover, at its peak in 1683, North and North East Africa, Eastern Europe, Greece and most of the Middle East. As it expanded into the heartland of the Islamic faith it became the effective protector of Sunni Islam, with both Mecca and Medina within its territory.

The Empire was forced to undergo a series of modernising reforms through the course of the nineteenth century in order to counter increasing nationalist movements among the provinces under its control and to keep military and economic pace with the Western Powers. At this time the Ottoman Empire was largely agrarian. It was common practice to trade with other nations to import products which the Empire did not make for itself and by this means the merchants of England and Holland had grown rich from trading into Ottoman lands. The state was the single largest landowner and derived its income from those lands. By the nineteenth century, central control over the Empire was weakening and many provincial lands were reverting to private ownership, where they weren't simply stripped away by treaties following disastrous wars against foreign powers. The removal of land detracted from the Empire's source of income.

The elites of the Empire had realised that the traditional government and sharia law by which the Empire was governed was not comparable to Britain, Austria and Russia. The Empire had fallen behind the major European powers by the mid-nineteenth century which left it vulnerable to attack. This was particularly the case with Russia which whom the Ottoman Empire shared an extensive border. The territory had already been lost at the end of the eighteenth century following wars with Russia and Austria. As a result of these treaties, the Crimean Khanate gained its independence as did the European regions of Moravia and Wallachia. Meanwhile, Arab tribal leaders on the Arabian peninsula were also in revolt, effectively ending Ottoman control of the region.

The legal system of the old regime in the Ottoman Empire was based on two systems; Sultanic Law (which resided with the Sultan as the ultimate authority) and Shari'a law. The Ottoman legal system had for a long time recognised three distinct groups of subjects; Muslims, dhimmis (Christians and Jews) and musta'mins (non-Muslim foreigners living within the Empire). All residents of the Empire were expected to fall into one of these three categories, with their religion a dominant factor. But the Ottoman Empire was an incredibly diverse state covering a huge geographical area and comprising countless different ethnic and religious groups.

By the nineteenth century, these groups were starting to see themselves as more than the limiting definitions of the state allowed for. Inspired by the French Revolution, there was a growing nationalist movement accompanied by an increasing desire for self-determination and independence from the Ottoman state.

12.2 - The beginnings of reform

Reform began with Sultan Mustafa III (ruled 1757 to 1773). He began to carry out reforms of the Ottoman military necessary to gain victory over Russia during a protracted war (fought from 1768 - 1774). This included reform of the artillery corps and the formation of a Naval academy. The Russo-Turkish War ended disastrously for the Ottoman Empire with the loss of territory in the Crimea, Romania and parts of Bulgaria. He was succeeded in 1789 by his son Selim III. The new Sultan was also reformist in his outlook. He began to modernise the Empire and continued with his father's military reforms. The priority of the Empire enabled the Ottomans to defend their territory against technologically superior foes, such as Russia. To this end, he continued to create military academies for the army and naval engineering. He began a foreign policy of engagement in order to seek out powerful allies, altering the policy of isolationism which had been the practice to that point.

Military reforms were significant in the Ottoman state not simply as a means of defence. It was a necessary part of undermining one of the strongest vested interests in Ottoman society. For centuries the elite of the Ottoman army had been the Janissary, the royal bodyguard. Beginning as soldiers recruited as boys from Christian slaves, they became a social clique at court wielding significant political power over the Sultans because of the privileged access to the royal person afforded to a bodyguard. They became landowners and wealthy men in their own right. By the time of Selim III, the Janissaries were one of the more entrenched conservative groups, actively hostile to any reform that would challenge their social and political pre-eminence. More than one Sultan had been removed from his throne by the Janissary to protect their own power and influence. The reform agenda of Selim III involved changing the army to the European model of a professional standing army, and this threatened the elite status of the Janissary.

This wasn't the only aspect of Imperial society which Selim wanted to reform, though all of his reforms ultimately came back to the same goal; to strengthen his regime against external and internal threats. To this end he founded the New Order army, to counter the Janissaries. He created the means of training specialists for his New Order at the army and navy academies. Selim III also set up an infrastructure allowing for primary and secondary education up to university levels, to be provided by the state. Previously, education had been in the hands of the ulema, Islamic clerical elite. The ulama were another vested interest in Ottoman society, occupying a high position and reaping the benefits. They too would form a group keen to undermine any Sultan who sought to reform.

It was the attempts to reform the army which led to the downfall of Selim III. The New Order began to be formed in 1797 and drew its recruits from Turkish peasantry. It grew to 23,000 strong, including artillery units and proved effective when deployed. The Janissaries saw the new force as a threat to their independence and elite position. The Ulema objected to the Western, European nature of the New Order, which was led by European officers.

In 1807, Selim III was overthrown and executed by the Janissary, to be replaced by Sultan Mustafa IV, who was opposed to reform. But this didn't stop the modernisation movement. The Janissaries rioted in Constantinople in a desire to root out any supporters of Selim III. A general in support of Selim III, Mustafa Bayrakdar led his force of 40,000 men and marched on Constantinople in an attempt to save the Sultan. Bayrakdar was an advocate of the reformist agenda. He arrived in the city too late to save Selim III, who had been murdered. Instead, Bayrakdar pursued vengeance against those who had deposed Selim and in particular the Janissary, who were running amuck in the streets of Constantinople. He was able to eliminate the Janissary forces and restore order in Constantinople. Mustafa IV, a conservative, was promptly deposed after reigning for only ten days. Bayrakdar caused the son of Selim III, Mahmud II, to be raised to the Sultanate. Memud shared both his father's and grandfather's passion for reform and would continue this work and deepen its scope.

12.3 - The Tanzimat

Mehmud continued the work of his father. First, he obtained a fatwa (a religious command issued by the clerical elite - the ulema) against the Janissary. They had done to same against his father to justify their overthrow of him. The ulema had, on the whole, not been supporters of reform but some believed that the Janissary gave preferential treatment to Non-Muslims because of their historic Christian origins (the first Janissary corps was made up of boys recruited from Christian slaves). The Janissary was finally and officially abolished in June 1826, following careful planning by the Sultan. Mehmud used his grandfather's New Order troops to surround the Janissary barracks and fired on it with artillery when the Janissary was about to mount a further protest against his reform agenda. The action Mahmud II took, effectively crushed the Janissary once and for all. It was a significant step in the reformist movement and its importance can't be understated. The Janissary had been a barrier to change for more than two generations and a weapon held to the throat of any Sultan desiring to see change. Though the Ulema had taken Mahmud's side against the Janissary, they had allied themselves in the opposite direction for his father Selim III. Without the military supremacy of the Janissary, the reform agenda could be moved on without fear of effective armed opposition.

Mahmud II's reforms were based on the administration of the Empire. He increased the reach of the central authority over Ottoman territory and continued the practice of opening academies and engineering schools. Unlike his father, however, he insisted that the language of these schools be Arabic-Turkish (Selim had recruited French instructors and made French the language of education).

Mehmud believed in westernising the Empire and under his reign, Westernisation became a formal policy. This included the bureaucracy, which was reshaped to match the Western civil service's. Even Western clothing was adopted, with the military taking on European-style uniforms.

Mehmud would die in 1839, but his successor Abdul Mejid attempted to deepen his father's reform work.

Abdul Mejid I would pass a decree known as the Tanzimat. It included lifelong property rights of citizens, guaranteed. The prohibition of bribery and formal regulation of taxation. A series of laws were passed known as the 'Canun' which would gradually replace the traditional shari'a law. The core principles of the Tanzimat were;

- All subjects should have their lives and property protected

- Taxes should be fairly imposed and justice impartially delivered

- Full religious equality and civil rights for all subjects.

A Council of Ministers was created as one of the first acts of the Tanzimat era. Its members were chosen by the Sultan and they were effectively an extension of his executive power. But it was the first step in the democratisation of the Ottoman state as the members of the Council of Ministers could influence policy through their control over which legislation was put before the Sultan for enactment.

The Tanzimat sought to begin to separate Church and state. It began to secularise education through the Public Education Law of 1839. It also ended the 'Millet' system by which all Ottoman subjects were grouped based on their religion. The reforms and modernising agenda of the Tanzimat would continue for the next thirty years until the late 1870's and the rule of Abdul Hamid II (grandson of Abdul Mejid I). Under his rule, the Tanzimat would ultimately come to an end but not before a brief moment in which the government of the Empire was transformed.

12.4 - The Young Ottomans

The group which would become known as the Young Ottomans were a secret society of liberal intellectuals formed in 1865. They believed that the reforms of the Tanzimat did not go far enough and that what was needed was a constitutional government, along European lines, with a Parliamentary democracy but underpinned by shari'a law. They had all worked in the Ottoman bureaucracy and had first-hand knowledge of both how the Empire operated and how other European states did. They also had access to publications and finance by which means they could make their views public.

Between 1873 and 1878 a series of crises struck the Ottoman Empire. A drought, followed by floods in Anatolia in 1873 and 1874 caused the government to raise taxes to make up the lost income. This led to discontent amongst the people which culminated in a series of revolts by Christian peasants in Serbia, Bosnia and Bulgaria. In the repression of the Bulgarian revolt, the Ottomans were accused of brutality and this led to a war against Russia (at the head of an alliance comprising Bulgaria and other Balkan states).

The war proved disastrous for the Ottomans. Bulgaria, Bosnia, Serbia, Montenegro and Cyprus were all lost to the Empire, either to full independence or being snapped up by other European powers (Austria took Bosnia and Britain took Cyprus). It was a humiliation for the Ottomans and led to discontent among the Muslim population. The government was seen to be appeasing foreign powers with its Westernising policies and the treaty which had ended the Russo-Turkish War. Increasingly, the views of the Young Ottomans were finding support in the streets of Constantinople.

On 30th May 1876, Sultan Abdul Aziz was overthrown in a coup. He was replaced by his nephew Murad, who was a close supporter of the Young Ottomans. His mental health rapidly deteriorated however and he was replaced by Abdul Hamid II. In 1876 the new Sultan enacted a constitution that began the First Constitutional Era. It would appear, however, that this was merely an attempt to appease visiting European leaders rather than a serious desire for reform along the lines that the Young Ottomans wanted to see. In 1878, constitution and Parliament both were abolished.

The reign of Abdul Aziz would continue until 1908. But the brief moment of the Young Ottomans in achieving their goal of a Parliamentary democracy and a constitutional government would not be forgotten. It would be remembered by another group of young rebels who would bring about the downfall of the Sultan, these would be known as the Young Turks.

12.5 - The Young Turks

Sultan Abdul Hamid faced opposition to his more conservative policies and his anti-reform agenda from the outset of his reign. The Young Ottomans represented the middle ground amongst the young intellectuals emerging from Istanbul University. They were socially and politically liberal while retaining a conservative religious outlook. The Young Turks emerged in the 1870's from progressive university students at the University of Istanbul. Notables of the Young Turk movement at this point were Mehmet Bey, Nuri Bey and Namik Kemal. They found their movement suppressed in 1876 by the Sultan and fled to Paris in exile. There the continued their opposition to the Sultan while continuing to operate as an underground group in the Empire itself.

The name they chose for their underground operations was the Committee of Union and Progress. It formed an intellectual opposition which included other groups discontented by the direction in which the country was going. They believed in science and reason above religion. For this reason, they adopted as their policy, Pan-Turkism over Pan-Ottomanism or even Pan-Islamism. They were focused on the concept of Turkish nationalism, fearing that the Empire had gone too far towards international appeasement. Their views found support among other Turks who felt disenfranchised by the current administration. It was in the Macedonian city of Salonica that the CUP found it's heartland. The CUP members in Salonica were mostly army members. In a country where democracy as a concept was still relatively young, it is no surprise that opposition crystallised in the military.

In 1908 supporters of CUP revolted. Imperial forces sent to crush the rebellion ended up joining them. The regime collapsed and Sultan Abdul Hamid became a constitutional ruler almost overnight. He capitulated to the CUP demands on 23rd July and by the 24th July, the CUP was proclaiming the release of all political prisoners, the end of censorship and the restoration of the Constitution of 1876. While the 1876 revolution became known as the First Constitutional Era so the 1908 uprising was the Second. In November 1908, elections were held and 280 deputies were elected. All male subjects over twenty-five were eligible to vote. For deputies, the only restriction on standing for Parliament was the ability to speak Turkish. The Sultan officially opened Parliament on December 17th, 1908. It was a democratic government and a secular one. Muslims and Non-Muslims alike were eligible to vote.

A counter-revolution was launched on 13th April 1909, comprising some members of the army, ulema and other conservatives who sought a return to shari'a law. The coup was successful and the Sultan was restored to a position of absolute power. Meanwhile, all non-Muslim deputies were ordered to leave their positions in Parliament. In a conservative backlash, some ten thousand Christian Armenians were massacred in the province of Adana in 1909. This was during a ten-day coup by Hamidian loyalists, who managed to seize Istanbul briefly. In that time the massacre occurred against the Christian Armenian population who had begun to arm themselves and organise politically, upon hearing of the overthrow of the Sultan.

The CUP response was swift however and the 3rd Army marched out of Salonica for Istanbul, led by Mustafa Kemal, Enver Pasa and Ismet Inonu. They would exact a bloody repression on all dissenters, capturing the Sultan and sending him into exile. These men saw themselves as the saviours of the Empire. One of their principle policies was to end the European interference in the Empire's internal affairs. The CUP pursued a Turkish nationalism rather than Ottoman as they realised that Non-Muslims were increasingly resistance to a call to arms from a Muslim Sultan, but could identify with a Turkish nationality which was divorced from Arabism and Islam. The Young Turks may have instituted a Parliamentary democracy, and limited the power of the Sultan greatly, but they demonstrated early on that their desire to consolidate their power was more important than the freedom and liberty they had espoused while in opposition.

The motto of the CUP had been an echo of the French Revolution 'Liberty, Equality, Fraternity and Justice'. This is likely to be part of a propaganda campaign to distinguish themselves from the establishment. Amongst the promises of the Young Turks was political parties to replace the old houses and religious elites in government. A free press was also promised along with a democratically elected Parliament. These promises were short-lived. Initially, opposition groups were allowed, with the Freedom and Accord party forming in 1911 and winning a by-election in Istanbul. The reaction to this by the CUP was to rig the general election of 1912. Their victorious government was ousted by a group of partisan army officers and the Freedom and Accord party were able to form a government under their leader Kamil Pasha.

12.6 - The Coup d'etat of 1913

The states of Greece, Montenegro, Bulgaria and Serbia had all won their independence from the Ottoman Empire in the later years of the nineteenth century. But all of these fledgeling nations possessed large numbers of Turkish population who remained under Ottoman rule. Now those Balkan nations banded together against the Ottomans. The outcome was a disaster for the Turks and is still bemoaned as a humiliating chapter in Turkish history. All of the Empire's European territories, west of Turkey, were lost to the Balkan League. It was during the peace negotiations from the First Balkan War that members of the CUP staged a coup known as the Raid on the Sublime Porte (the Sublime Porte was the home of Ottoman government in Istanbul).

This took place on January 23rd, 1913 and resulted in the resignation of Kamil Pasha and the assassination of Minister of the Navy, Nazim Pasha. The leaders of the coup were Enver Pasha, Talaat Pasha and Djemal Pasha. These three would form a triumvirate that would lead the new Ottoman government. The CUP had regained power and showed no signs of risking defeat. They set upon a program of eliminating political opposition.

This began with the closure of Parliament in 1913. There followed a campaign of political assassinations was begun against key opponents. Political opposition was crushed despite the promise to allow political parties and a free press. The Young Turk movement themselves had flourished in opposition thanks to the free press of other European nations, such as France. Now the party which that revolution had produced was prepared to rule as dictators in order to secure their position.

Between 1912 and 1918, the CUP ruled unopposed. The Sultan they had chosen to replace Abdul Hamid, Mehmed V was largely a figurehead with no effective power at all. Real power lay with a triumvirate of 'Pashas'. Pasha was the honorary title gained by military officers upon achieving the rank of Major General. Enver Pasha was appointed Minister of War on January 4th, 1914. Alongside him was Talaat Pasha who held the office of Grand Vizier (prime minister) and Djemal Pasha (Minister for the Navy). There brutal repression of political opposition may have been born of a desire to consolidate their power and build a strong, central government for the floundering Empire. The early years of the twentieth century was a turbulent time, particularly in eastern and central Europe. The European powers of Britain, France, Germany and Austro-Hungary were each manoeuvring for position and influence, with smaller nations falling into a network of alliances and treaties to avoid being crushed in between.

Despite placing a greater emphasis on Pan-Turkism at the expense of Pan-Ottomanism (in other words attempting to rally the population around a secular, nationalist ideology) the CUP was still the government of what remained of the Ottoman Empire. Following the loss of Libya to the Italians in 1911 and European territory in the First Balkan War, the Ottoman Empire now allied itself to Germany. Germany was one of two European powers who desired to see the Empire remain intact, the other being Britain. Russia was a traditional enemy of the Ottomans and had sided with Balkan nationalism in order to increase its own influence in Eastern and Central Europe. This meant that it was in their interests to see the Empire broken apart. Meanwhile, the Austro-Hungarian Empire was fighting against the same Balkan nationalism that Russia encouraged, and which had cost the Ottomans dearly. The Austrian-Hungarians saw the Ottomans as similar to themselves in that they presided over a multinational empire. They wished to see the Ottomans remain strong in order to preserve their own position. It meant that the CUP government ended up placing the Empire into an alliance with what would become the Central powers during World War I.

12.7 - Dissolution of the Ottoman Empire

World War I marked the final end of the Ottoman Empire. With the defeat of the Central Powers, the victorious Allies sought to occupy and partition the Empire. This was resisted by a new nationalist movement led by a former Young Turk, Mustafa Kemal Ataturk. It was formed in 1919 as an independence movement against the powers that occupied Ottoman territory after the War. Under the terms of the Armistice, Ottoman territory was occupied and partitioned by the Greeks, Armenians, French and British. This included the partitioning of areas of Anatolia (modern day Turkey) which was the ancient heartland of the Ottoman nation. The Empire at this point was effectively dead but the Turkish Nationalist Movement, led by Ataturk, sought to hold together this heartland.

From May 19th, 1919 to July 24th, 1923, Ataturk led the Turkish Nationalist Movement in an armed conflict against the Allies and their proxy nations, such as Greece and Armenia, in an attempt to forge a new Turkish republic from the ashes of the Empire. This conflict came to be known as the Turkish War of Independence and was the logical successor to the Young Turk Revolution. The CUP had sought to overthrow the rule of the Sultan as an absolute monarch and revive the 1876 constitution. Though they had briefly achieved that, the resultant external crises which had threatened Ottoman integrity resulted in a reversion to a brutal, repressive state. Now, the successors of the Young Turks would lead a nationalist movement that would free the fledgeling Turkish republic from foreign intervention and finally abolish the Sultanate in 1922.

The new Turkish republic would be recognised internationally as the successor to the Ottoman Empire by the Treaty of Lausanne in July 1823.

12.8 - Aftermath

The Young Turk revolution was initially bloodless. It was a carefully planned coup with the power of the military behind it that forced the Sultan to recognise the need for change in order to preserve his throne. Their objective was to restore the constitution created in 1876 by the Young Ottomans which held the power of the monarch in check within a constitutional monarchy. Like many revolutionaries before them, the Young Turks, and the party which they formed, the CUP, promised many liberal reforms. The new Ottoman state would have political parties competing in free and fair elections, a free press and would be a secular state based on the common identity of Turkism, rather than an Islamic state in which non-Muslims were disenfranchised.

The reality of the power struggles of the early twentieth century Europe, however, meant that these lofty ideals could not be achieved. The Young Turks had promised to end the intervention in Ottoman affairs by foreign powers but were unable to achieve this in the build-up to World War I. No sooner had the Young Turks established their constitutional monarchy than a counter-revolution wrested control back. Though the counter-revolution seeking to restore the Sultan was ultimately defeated they succeeded in holding power long enough to carry out mass atrocities against the newly organised and politicised Christian population of Armenia. So while the 1908 revolution had been bloodless, it had set in motion a chain of events that would lead to the deaths of almost 100,000 Christian Armenians.

With the loss of Libya to the Italians and a humiliating defeat in the First Balkan War, the CUP decided to ensure it could not lose power again and began a policy of brutal repression of any political opposition. Parliament was dissolved and opposition leaders were targeted for assassination. After just four or five years of government led by a constitutional monarchy, the Ottoman state devolved once more to a dictatorship. This time ultimate power rested with three CUP leaders forming a triumvirate. They themselves would be ousted from power after choosing to ally the Ottoman Empire with the Central Powers during World War I.

The legacy of the Young Turks was the Turkish Nationalist Movement which was mobilised to fight the War of Independence. They were led by a former Young Turk, in Kemal Ataturk who would become the founding father of the Turkish Republic. The Nationalist Movement believed in preserving the 'Turkish' homeland at the heart of the old Ottoman Empire, forsaking any claims to Empire or an Islamic/Arabian political ideology. The Young Turks had been the first to realise that to pursue a philosophy based upon the Islamic nature of the Ottoman state (with the clerical elite occupying high positions and a Sultan as the ultimate authority) would not serve to weld together the disparate ethnic elements of the Empire. Their goal was nationalist solidarity through an ideology of Pan-Turkism.

In this pursuit, they failed. The Ottoman Empire could not withstand its alliance with the Central Powers in the First World War, nor the growing tide of nationalism sweeping the Balkan states. It ceased to exist as a nation following the war. Where the Young Turks were successful was in lighting the embers of Turkish nationalism that would be fanned to furious flames as the victorious Allies sought to dismember the old Ottoman Empire post-war.

The modern Turkish democracy is the ultimate legacy of the Young Turk revolution. It is a secular republic in which Islam is the dominant religion but which does not follow strict sharia law or consider itself a caliphate under an absolute monarch. The presence of Turkey in the east of Europe has provided NATO with a crucial ally against the Soviet Union and has proved pivotal in recent military actions in the Middle East. Turkey now serves as a bridge between the Islamic east and the secular west, a position which the old Ottoman state could not have occupied. World events in the last fifty years, and in particular in the last ten, would have been very different if not for the presence of a stable republic on borders of, first, the expansionist Soviet Union, and then the war-torn Middle East.

CHAPTER 13

SUMMARY

13.1 - Definitions of revolution

We have seen that the term revolution can be applied to any event which overturns the status quo, resulting in a completely new paradigm going forward. In political terms, this means the tearing down of the old system to replace it with a new, though this does not necessarily have to be a permanent change. A political revolution, as defined by Aristotle falls into two categories;

A complete change from one constitution to another

A modification of an existing constitution

Of the revolutions which we have examined in this book, it can be shown that all fit one of these two definitions. But there are other definitions which must be applied.

13.2 - Mass uprising

A revolution must be a mass movement. It must involve an uprising of the mass of the population against the existing regime. This can be represented by a genuine, grassroots movement where the peasant classes themselves are the revolutionaries, such as the Haitian Revolution. In this instance, the black slaves of Saint Domingue rose behind a charismatic leader to overthrow their white, European overlords. Similarly, during the Cuban Revolution, another charismatic leader (Fidel Castro) would mobilise ordinary Cubans to fight against the American backed regime of Fulgencio Batista. In both cases, it was the people who formed the revolutionary forces and they pro-actively pursued their revolutionary agenda.

The mass uprising can also be one in which the mass of the people is a tool in the hands of a social or political elite group. The Iranian Revolution is an example of this. The regime of the Iranian Shah was not deposed by a 'People's army' or by mass riots instigated from within the working classes. Instead, the religious elite of Iranian society, the ulama, were the instigators. They whipped up the Iranian populace into an angry mob with which to attack the Shah and the infrastructure of the old regime. Similarly, the attempt by the 'Young Turks' of the Ottoman Empire to bring about a constitutional monarchy within their own country was not driven by a grassroots movement, but rather by military officers and an intellectual middle class.

Whether the mass uprising has been from a genuine desire by the people for change or from a social elite using the masses as a weapon; the end result is the same. This mass uprising against the old system is a prerequisite for a revolution.

13.3 - Political isolation

Another requirement which we have looked at is the isolation of the old regime, resulting in a disconnect between government and governed. This disconnect makes revolution easier in the minds of those seeking change, erasing any feeling of loyalty. It also makes it easier to break through generations of social programming which dictates that deference should be shown to social or political superiors (such as a monarch or a ruling elite).

This isolation can be in the form of an isolation from the common people or an isolation from the social and political elites instrumental in attaining and maintaining power. Of the former category, the communist revolutions of Russia and China are perfect examples. In both cases, a wealthy political and social elite (in both cases a monarchy) was physically divided from the mass of the people. Those masses lived a radically different life to those who ruled them. In the case of the Chinese, the Emperor lived in the Forbidden City, literally shut away from his people. These monarchs became remote to their people, symbols of a decadent elite whose wealth and prosperity was based on the hard work and suffering of the ordinary people.

By contrast, during the Glorious Revolution which occurred in England in 1689, it wasn't the mass of the English populace that precipitated the abdication of King James II (though there would have been mass protests and even riots in the streets of London, whipped up by the King's opponents). Instead, this revolution was instigated by Parliament to prevent the possibility of a Catholic dynasty on the English throne. This was the same social and political group that had restored the monarchy to the throne in 1660, following eleven years in which England was a republic. King James II isolated himself from this crucial political elite through his choice of religion and his unwillingness to compromise on this issue. The result was that he was forced to abdicate and his throne was given away to William of Orange.

13.4 - Ideology

It takes a great deal of resolve to embark on the overthrowing of an entire political system, particularly if that is a monarchy that has governed without significant change for centuries. To be able to conceive that there is an alternative to the status quo, that suffering endured by the ordinary people is not simply part and parcel of life, requires a powerful change of mindset and considerable determination. This kind of change cannot conceivably be achieved without an overarching ideology behind it.

The ideology becomes an almost religious belief in the rightness of a cause and a justification for the suffering which must inevitably result from revolution. Without a strong ideological underpinning, there would surely be few revolutionaries prepared to go as far as is required to achieve their aims. In fact, without an ideology, there would be no revolutionary. There must be a system to replace that which has been overthrown. Ideology provides this.

For the Russians and Chinese is was Marxist socialism and subsequently Communism.

For the French, Americans and Haitians it was equality, liberty and democracy, a discarding of medieval European concepts such as royalty and aristocracy. For the Parliamentarians of England who set in motion the events that would see a King dethroned, it was motivated by similar beliefs, though their ideology was based around the preservation of the democratic system already in place and ensuring it could never be supplanted by a dictatorship.

For Cubans and 'Young Turks' the driving ideology was nationalism. Cuban people already had a democratic system (although Batiste had effectively dissolved it immediately prior to the start of Castro's war to supplant him) but it was one in which the United States possessed a great deal of political influence. A significant proportion of Cuba's economy was controlled by American businesses and a large chunk of the nation's wealth and land too.

What motivated the Cubans to follow Fidel Castro in his war to seize power was not, as the French third estate had done, a desire to win for themselves freedom and the right to participate in a democratic system. Castro's ideology was based on the primacy of Cuban nationalism. Cuba for Cubans, with the Cuban people the biggest beneficiaries of their own economy, not foreign businesses or governments. He wanted to see Cuba free from American interference or the threat of American invasion. Castro was also a socialist and once in power, this became a driving force in his belief structure, leading him to send Cuban advisors and troops to South America and Africa in an attempt to ferment socialist revolutions abroad. But during the revolution itself, nationalism was the driving force that brought the Cuban people together.

In the case of the group who would become known as the 'Young Turks' nationalism was the sole motivating ideology. These intellectuals and military officers saw their country (at that time the Ottoman Empire rather than the Republic of Turkey) as being eroded by foreign interference and by waves of ethnic nationalism in the territories that comprised this multiethnic and multinational empire. Countries gained their independence or were seized as spoils of war or as a result of treaties after a humiliating defeat. Each time this happened it weakened the Ottoman nation as a whole. The predominant philosophy of the ruling elite, the Sultans, was one of Pan-Islamism in which Muslims within the empire were given a position of superiority over non-muslims.

The 'Young Turks' saw that this psychology could not hold the nation together, as it did not bring the millions of non-Muslims together. It was the Arab / Islamic philosophy that drove the independence movements in regions such as the Balkans, where Muslims were in the minority. They sought to implement a new sense of Pan-Turkish nationalism that would weld the remaining Ottoman territories together more effectively.

Finally, we have the Iranian Revolution and Spanish Civil War. In both cases, there was a clear ideology driving the revolutionaries. But in both cases, the ideology was one of a return to the old regime. In Iran, this desire to undo change was driven by religious imperatives (or at least it was led by the religious elite whose position was threatened by secular reforms put in place by successive Shahs). In Spain, the nationalist forces led by Franco were seeking to put an end to republicanism. For the Spanish nationalists, this meant restoring the Spain which had existed, unchanged, for centuries up to the point where the Republicans had seized power. It meant restoring the power and supremacy of the Catholic church and undoing land reforms, which had empowered a peasant class that had been effectively living in a state of serfdom.

While the ideologies driving these two instances of revolution can only be described as counter-revolutionary (seeking as they did to undo the changes brought about by previous reforms or revolutions) nevertheless these movements tore down the status quo and both were driven by a strong ideological belief in the rightness of their cause.

13.5 - Aristotle's Definitions

So, all of our revolutions fit the definitions of mass uprising, whether an uprising driven by the people or in which the masses of the people are being used as a weapon. We have also seen how each is motivated by an ideology. All of the revolutions we have examined fall into one of Aristotle's definitions;

The French Revolution - The French Revolution left nothing recognisable from the 'ancien regime' in its wake. Even the people who had comprised the social and political elites of French society in the old regime were gone. The Revolutionaries zeal for change was such that royals, clergy and aristocrats were executed en masse. What replaced the old regime was something that had not existed before. The revolutionaries composed a new constitution which put forward unalienable rights and liberties, guaranteeing equality. Such concepts were foreign to the French society that had existed to that point.

The American Revolution - the American revolution also fits the first definition thought the American colonists were fighting for their independence from what they saw as a foreign power rather than attempting to overthrow an internal governmental system. The Americans did, however, formulate their own unique system of government underpinned by a constitution that deliberately cast aside the inequalities of the European social order. The American colonists did not have the right to cast votes in the British Parliamentary democracy but they, as subjects of the Crown, were given some of the liberties and rights of Englishmen. These rights and liberties had themselves been won in 1689 during the Glorious Revolution when the English had secured their own freedoms from the arbitrary whims of absolute monarchy.

Indeed, it could be argued that the American revolution was not so radical in that it was seeking to replace a Parliamentary democracy with another form of democratic constitution. The key point is that the Americans did not possess the right to vote in the British system though they were still subject to taxation. The political and social system which the fledgeling United States represented in 1776 was something completely new, discarding concepts such as aristocracy and royalty in favour of equality.

The Russian Revolution - The Russian 'October' revolution is another archetypal example of a complete change to the status quo. As the French did in 1789, the Russian peasant classes were politicised and mobilised to overthrow a wealthy elite. The Russian system prior to the revolution was a model of inequality, with abject poverty and starvation, the lot of the working people, many of whom lived in almost medieval conditions of serfdom. This was in stark contrast to the wealth and opulence enjoyed by the Czars at the apex of Russian society.

When the revolution came the system which replaced the Czarist absolute monarchy was one that had never been seen before in world history. In the case of the French, they could take their inspiration from the Americans. The Americans could take their inspiration from the British at least in broad general terms. But there had been no true socialist revolutions before and not socialist states. The philosophy which drove the Bolsheviks was one that had only been conceived in the late nineteenth century by Karl Marx. The inspiration which drove Lenin and Stalin was one that was new to the human consciousness. The state which Lenin built to replace Czarist Russia was equally as novel. It could not be anything else.

The Chinese Communist Revolution - The revolutions that overthrew the Qing dynasty in China in the twentieth century were also inspired by Marxism and ultimately produced a society just as alien when compared to what had gone before. Mao personally decided that his new world should be an overnight change to what had gone before. This was something that Stalin too believed in. To institute a constitutional change overnight is something that can be achieved quite easily. Once the institutions of government are seized, along with all the mechanisms of the state, a revolutionary can create any written constitution they desire and declare it valid the second the ink is dry. Alternatively, it can be voted into existence with a show of hands. This was the overnight change achieved by the French and the Americans. Where the Russians and Chinese differ, or rather where Josef Stalin and Mao Tse Tung differ, is that they attempted to create entirely new societies overnight.

Both wished to move their traditional agrarian economies to an industrial base, practically overnight. Change on this scale cannot be achieved with a great deal of upheaval. It could be argued that the Great Leap Forward, as Mao entitled his attempt to make China industrial overnight in 1958, was more brutal and destabilising than the conflict which had brought the Communists to power, or the revolutions prior to the Communist takeover that had overthrown the Qing Emperor. Stalin attempted the same by collectivising all Russian farms and converting the economy to heavy industry. Both resulted in widespread famine and suffering on an incredible scale, with a death toll reaching into the millions.

Both Russian and Chinese communist revolutions then are textbook definitions of the complete change from one constitution to another as defined by Aristotle. In both cases, the communist state which replaced the old regime was completely new. But, crucially, both featured an attempt to transform the nature of the state in the most radical way possible (from agrarian to industrial) and so are the very definition of revolutionary.

It is worth highlighting the Taiping revolution while discussing those revolutions which completely transformed their societies;

Taiping Revolution - the attempted revolution of the Heavenly Kingdom of Taiping was a failed revolution. This revolution centred around the self-proclaimed messiah Hong Xiuquan and his attempt to destroy the Manchu political elite that had governed China for three hundred years. There can be no doubt that for a period of time it seemed Xiuquan's attempt to create a Christian state within China was successful. This goal certainly fits the definition of revolutionary, seeking as it did to overthrow the three-thousand-year-old Confucian philosophy that had been preeminent in China to that point. While the Taiping never managed to overthrow the Qing dynasty they did bring about a revolution within the territory they captured. Ultimately, though, the Taiping armies were defeated by the vested interests in Chinese society (with the support of

Western powers protecting their own commercial interests) and their revolution failed. Had it succeeded it would have led to as radical a change to Chinese society as could be imagined.

The Haitian Revolution - Though not as well known to the mainstream of history readers, nevertheless the Haitian revolution (or the Saint Domingue revolution as Haiti only became the name of the new nation once it had won its independence) is a textbook example of the first of Aristotle's definitions. This was the rising of a black slave population against a wealthy, militarised and vastly more populous European empire. While the white French on the island of Saint Domingue were outnumbered by the vast numbers of African slaves they had imported to fuel their cash crop economy, there was a vast reservoir of manpower throughout the empire which could be brought to bear. Despite the seemingly overwhelming odds, the slaves of Saint Domingue succeeded in bringing about their own liberation.

Not only did they achieve freedom from slavery but they also secured the independence of their land from the French empire. Following the massacre of whites on the island and the declaration of the independent state of Haiti, this freedom had to be bought with the payments of reparations to the French state (with the threat of invasion should payments not be maintained). But despite this the Saint Domingue slaves did succeed in completely overturning the system of government under which they had been slaves.

The Cuban Revolution - Cuba possessed a healthy and growing economy and a democratic system of government prior to Castro's revolt. The democratic institutions were corrupt and the economy was being exploited in the interests of American businesses at the expense of ordinary Cubans. This provided a fertile ground for Castro's nationalist and socialist ideology which sought a Cuba free from the interference of the United States and in which Cuban workers could benefit from their own productivity.

It should be noted that the system of government which Castro replaced was, by the time of the revolution, a dictatorship. President Batiste had dissolved the democratic apparatus and cancelled elections in order to preserve his own power. Castro would replace Batiste as a dictator. So, in one sense there was no change to the actual governance of Cuba. The Cuban people were still not free to democratically elect their own representatives or leaders and were forced to live under an effective military dictatorship. Where the Cuban Revolution can be said to fit Aristotle's first definition is that Castro succeeded in removing the influence of American businesses and eliminating the political and military domination of the United States over Cuba.

The Castro regime would nationalise all Cuban industry and subsequently collectivise all private property as Castro adopted a fully communist ideology. This was an overthrow of the capitalist economy that Cuba had possessed prior to the revolution. Castro can even be said to have reversed the promising economic growth which had been achieved under Cuba's period of being exploited by America. By removing private property Castro succeeded in removing the motivation of the Cuban workforce to be productive. Industries that had previously been successful began to slow down or even fail. The Cuban economy went into a decades-long period of stagnation until the beginnings of the tourist economy from the 1990's onwards.

That brings us to the second of Aristotle's definitions;

To modify an existing constitution

This definition serves to encompass the remainder of our revolutions.

The Glorious Revolution - there is no claim that the English Parliament sought a radical new constitution following the abdication of King James II. In fact, the idea of overturning the English political system, the fledgeling constitutional monarchy that already existed would not have been in their interests. Instead, what they sought was to codify the constitutional monarchy system by producing a Bill of Rights which the monarch would be a signatory to. They created the political system which survives to this day and which was a small change to what had gone before. The main difference was the formalising of what had previously been non-written conventions.

The Iranian Revolution - while from one viewpoint the Ayatollah did seek to completely overthrow the Iranian monarchy, replacing it with a theocracy. On another hand, it could be argued that the theocratic government which the Iranian revolution produced was not a novel system. It was rather a return to a previous state, where the Islamic clerics held a position of social and political power. The only difference in the state which emerged from the Iranian revolution was the removal of the monarch. The religious elites which were responsible for the downfall of the Shah were, by their very nature, conservative. They abhorred the concept of change and reform. Instead, they were motivated by a desire to return to a traditional way of life.

The Spanish Civil War - This desire to restore a previous 'golden age' is at the heart of the Spanish Civil War and the counter-revolutionary movement of Franco's nationalists. As has been mentioned under Ideology, Franco believed in the restoration of a traditional Spain, with the Catholic Church at the heart of the nation and a rigid social hierarchy based on lineage and land ownership. While the Nationalists defeat of Republicanism caused the Republican system to be completely overturned, that system had not been fully embedded into Spanish society and itself represents a brief moment of limited change.

The Young Turks - the last of our revolutions was a movement that did not seek to replace the leadership of the Sultan, nor to overthrow the traditional methods of government. The rebels looked instead for reform as part of a constitutional monarchy. They deposed a Sultanate, who they saw as being opposed to reform and modernisation and replaced him with one more amenable to change. But they did not look to abolish the Sultan as the head of state.

13.6 - Conclusion

Revolutions, based on the study of those revolts examined here, are by their very nature a cause for much bloodshed and suffering, typically amongst the very lowest in a given society. Because revolutions are mass uprisings, they are aimed at improving the lives of those people who end up suffering the most. It is debatable whether there is a long-term benefit which outweighs the short or medium term upheaval and loss of life.

France has become one of the most successful Western European democracies and its people now enjoy all the freedoms and equality that are associated with a modern day, western democracy. However, that freedom was bought at the cost of extreme violence in the revolutionary period followed by decades of warfare as France sought to export its revolutions.

The Glorious Revolution of England was supposedly bloodless, hence the name. However, the victory of a Protestant monarch against a Catholic who sought to restore his throne with an Irish army has left divisions in Britain and Ireland which continue to this day. With Britain's imminent departure from the European Union, this problem has become even more relevant as the debate over the border between Northern Ireland and the Republic of Ireland threatens to derail the hard-won peace of the 1990's. There is a clear path from the Battle of the Boyne in 1690, where Protestant defeated Catholic to the sectarian divisions within modern-day Northern Ireland and Western Scotland.

In the case of the Russian and Chinese Communist revolutions, the death tolls run into the tens if not hundreds of millions. In Russia, the revolution spawned a failed Soviet state that caused suffering to its own citizens as well as fear throughout the world for its nuclear rivalry with the United States. However, in the final aftermath, Russia now has a stable democracy (albeit one that appears dominated by oligarchs and alleged corruption) and the massive class inequality that had existed under the Czar's is no more. China continues to operate a communist state and an effective dictatorship though has forged one of the world's most successful economies and an improved standard of living for many ordinary Chinese.

Most readers of this book would surely agree that slavery is an evil institution and a revolution that brings about the freedom of slaves must be seen as good. However, the Haitian slave revolt resulted in one of the world's poorest nations. The revolution required the elimination of all those people who understood how best to leverage Haiti's plantation economy.

The former slaves who took control of their own destiny found they lacked the skills to manage a self-sufficient economy. They were hampered by the reactionary views and racism of the rest of the world, who refused to recognise or trade with the new nation, but the ferocity of the revolutionary violence played its part. This violence frightened nations who could have helped Haiti, such as the United States and Britain, because of the slave economies which both nations still relied upon.

Had the Haitians not revolted they may well have been emancipated when Britain abolished the slave trade, especially given the proximity of Saint Domingue to the British colony of Jamaica. This may, in time have resulted in a more prosperous independent nation, given that France did ultimately relinquish all of its overseas colonies. Who can say how much an enslaved people should endure and for how long?

This question is replicated by the case of the Spanish Civil War. A Republican revolution would undoubtedly have been of benefit to the lowest classes of Spanish society. The Republicans can to power relatively bloodlessly too. However, their attempts to reform Spanish society for the betterment of ordinary Spanish people provoked a savage backlash from the right-wing nationalists. The violence they unleashed in their counter-revolution was truly terrible and resulted in a fascist, military dictatorship governing Spain for decades to come. Had the Republicans not attempted to overturn the status quo how might Spain have evolved? While the goals of the Republicans were laudable it is clear that for a highly motivated element of Spanish society the changes the Republicans sought was too much too soon.

Revolution, by its very nature, is a state of upheaval and disruption. It is simply a question of degree. Peaceful revolutions can have violent consequences just as violent revolutions can have ultimately peaceful results. Often it is necessary to long far along a nation's timeline to evaluate the impact of a revolution. The implications of the Glorious Revolution do not become evident until one reaches the twentieth century and Irish Independence. The success of the French Revolution isn't easy to see in the immediate aftermath but the eventual emergence of a modern, secular republic tells the tale. It is too simplistic to say that revolutions are a good or bad thing for human society. There is no question that great societal change for the good has arisen through revolution but the question remains of whether the ends justify the means.

ABOUT THE AUTHOR

Johnathan Kingsbury has been fascinated with history since childhood. An amateur historian, specializing in the study of ancient battlefields, his research has taken him to numerous battlefields that have marked pivotal moments throughout history, including Waterloo, Philippi, Normandy, The Ardennes, Gettysburg, and the Plains of Abraham. He lives in the Laurentians, Quebec with Scipio, his faithful Black Lab.

Lightning Source UK Ltd.
Milton Keynes UK
UKHW041814080319
338774UK00001B/179/P